Table of Contents

Smart Starts

Breakfast Rice Pudding

2 cups vanilla soymilk, divided
¾ cup quick-cooking brown rice*
⅓ cup packed brown sugar
½ teaspoon ground cinnamon
½ teaspoon salt
¼ cup golden raisins or dried sweetened cranberries (optional)
½ teaspoon vanilla
Mixed berries (optional)

*Look for rice that cooks in 20 to 25 minutes. For rice with a longer cooking time, increase the cooking time in step 1.

1. Bring 1½ cups soymilk to a simmer in medium saucepan over medium-high heat. Stir in rice, brown sugar, cinnamon and salt. Reduce heat to low; cover and simmer 10 minutes.

2. Stir in remaining ½ cup soymilk and raisins, if desired; cover and simmer 10 minutes. Remove from heat; stir in vanilla. Serve with berries, if desired.

Makes 4 servings

Note: Rice thickens as it cools. For a thinner consistency, stir in additional soymilk just before serving.

Crispy Skillet Potatoes ❯

> 2 tablespoons olive oil
> 4 red potatoes, cut into thin wedges
> ½ cup chopped onion
> 2 tablespoons lemon pepper
> ½ teaspoon coarse salt
>   Chopped fresh parsley (optional)

1. Heat oil in large skillet over medium heat. Stir in potatoes, onion, lemon pepper and salt.

2. Cover and cook 25 to 30 minutes or until potatoes are tender and browned, turning occasionally. Sprinkle with parsley just before serving.

Makes 4 servings

Tofu Peanut Butter Smoothie

> 1 banana, cut into chunks
> 4 ounces soft tofu
> ¼ cup creamy peanut butter
> 1 tablespoon sugar
> 1 to 2 ice cubes
> 1 teaspoon vanilla

Combine banana, tofu, peanut butter, sugar, ice and vanilla in blender; blend until smooth. Serve immediately.

Makes 1 (8-ounce) serving

Oatmeal with Maple Glazed Apples and Cranberries

3 cups water

2 cups quick or old-fashioned oats

¼ teaspoon salt

1 tablespoon dairy-free margarine

2 medium unpeeled Red or Golden Delicious apples, cut into ½-inch chunks

¼ teaspoon ground cinnamon

2 tablespoons maple syrup

4 tablespoons dried cranberries

Slow Cooker Directions

1. Combine water, oats and salt in slow cooker. Cover; cook on LOW 8 hours.

2. Just before serving, melt margarine in large nonstick skillet over medium heat. Add apples and cinnamon; cook and stir 4 to 5 minutes or until tender. Stir in maple syrup; cook until heated through.

3. Spoon oatmeal into four bowls; top with apple mixture and dried cranberries.

Makes 4 servings

Superfoods Smoothie ❯

> **1 cup packed stemmed kale**
> **1 cup baby spinach**
> **1 cup ice cubes**
> **1 banana**
> **½ cup apple juice**

Combine kale, spinach, ice, banana and apple juice in blender; blend until smooth.

Makes 2 (6-ounce) servings

French Toast Sticks

> **1 cup vanilla soymilk**
> **3 tablespoons all-purpose flour**
> **½ teaspoon ground cinnamon**
> **½ teaspoon vanilla**
> **1 rectangular loaf unsliced French bread (16 ounces)**
> **1 to 2 tablespoons dairy-free margarine**
> **Powdered sugar**
> **Maple syrup**

1. Whisk soymilk, flour, cinnamon and vanilla in large bowl until well blended.

2. Cut bread into 12 (4×1×1-inch) pieces.

3. Melt 1 tablespoon margarine on large nonstick griddle or in large skillet over medium-high heat. Dip bread pieces in soymilk mixture to coat. Cook about 5 minutes or until golden brown on all sides, adding additional margarine if needed. Dust lightly with powdered sugar; serve with maple syrup.

Makes 4 servings

Breakfast Quinoa

½ cup uncooked quinoa
1 cup water
1 tablespoon packed brown sugar
2 teaspoons maple syrup
½ teaspoon ground cinnamon
¼ cup golden raisins (optional)
   Dairy-free milk
   Fresh raspberries and banana slices

1. Place quinoa in fine-mesh strainer; rinse well under cold running water. Transfer to small saucepan.

2. Stir in 1 cup water, brown sugar, maple syrup and cinnamon; bring to a boil over high heat. Reduce heat to low; cover and simmer 10 to 15 minutes or until quinoa is tender and water is absorbed. Add raisins, if desired, during last 5 minutes of cooking. Serve with dairy-free milk; top with raspberries and bananas.

Makes 2 servings

Note: Quinoa may seem new to many Americans but it is actually an ancient grain that was grown by the Incas. This tiny round whole grain is higher in protein than other grains and contains all eight essential amino acids, so it is considered a complete protein.

Scrambled Tofu and Potatoes

Potatoes

> ¼ cup olive oil
>
> 4 to 5 red potatoes, cubed
>
> ½ white onion, sliced
>
> 1 tablespoon chopped fresh rosemary
>
> 1 teaspoon coarse salt

Scrambled Tofu

> ¼ cup nutritional yeast
>
> ½ teaspoon ground turmeric
>
> 2 tablespoons water
>
> 2 tablespoons soy sauce
>
> 1 package (14 ounces) firm tofu
>
> 2 teaspoons olive oil
>
> ½ cup chopped green bell pepper
>
> ½ cup chopped red onion

1. For potatoes, preheat oven to 450°F. Pour ¼ cup olive oil into large cast iron skillet; place skillet in oven 10 minutes to heat.

2. Bring large saucepan of water to a boil. Add potatoes; cook 5 to 7 minutes or until fork-tender. Drain potatoes and return to saucepan; stir in white onion, rosemary and salt. Spread mixture in preheated skillet. Bake 25 to 30 minutes or until potatoes are browned, stirring every 10 minutes.

3. For tofu, combine nutritional yeast and turmeric in small bowl. Stir in water and soy sauce until smooth.

4. Cut tofu into eight cubes. Gently squeeze out water; loosely crumble tofu into medium bowl. Heat 2 teaspoons olive oil in large skillet over medium-high heat. Add bell pepper and red onion; cook and stir 2 minutes or until soft but not browned. Add tofu; drizzle with 3 tablespoons nutritional yeast sauce. Cook and stir about 5 minutes or until liquid is evaporated and tofu is uniformly colored and heated through. Stir in additional sauce, if desired, for stronger flavor.

5. Divide potatoes among four serving plates. Top with tofu.

Makes 4 servings

Super Oatmeal ❯

2 cups water
2¾ cups old-fashioned oats
½ cup finely diced dried figs
⅓ cup packed dark brown sugar
½ cup sliced almonds, toasted*
¼ cup flaxseeds
½ teaspoon salt
½ teaspoon ground cinnamon
2 cups dairy-free milk

To toast almonds, spread in single layer on baking sheet. Bake in preheated 350°F oven 8 to 10 minutes or until golden brown, stirring frequently.

1. Bring water to a boil in large saucepan over high heat. Stir in oats, figs, brown sugar, almonds, flax seeds, salt and cinnamon. Immediately add dairy-free milk; mix well.

2. Reduce heat to medium; cook and stir 5 to 7 minutes or until oatmeal is thick and creamy. Spoon into individual bowls.

Makes 4 to 6 servings

Pear Avocado Smoothie

1½ cups ice cubes
1 pear, peeled and cubed
1 cup apple juice
½ avocado, peeled and pitted
½ cup fresh mint leaves
2 tablespoons fresh lime juice

Combine ice, pear, apple juice, avocado, mint and lime juice in blender; blend until smooth. Serve immediately.

Makes 2 (8- to 10-ounce) servings

Vegan Pancakes

2 cups soymilk or other dairy-free milk
2 tablespoons lemon juice
2 tablespoons vegetable oil
1 tablespoon agave nectar
1 cup all-purpose flour
1 cup spelt flour
1 teaspoon baking soda
1 teaspoon baking powder
½ teaspoon salt
1 to 2 tablespoons dairy-free magarine, melted
Fresh fruit and/or maple syrup

1. Combine soymilk and lemon juice in large measuring cup or medium bowl. Set aside 5 minutes. Stir in oil and agave.

2. Whisk all-purpose flour, spelt flour, baking soda, baking powder and salt in large bowl. Whisk in soymilk mixture until fairly smooth. (Some lumps will remain.)

3. Heat large nonstick skillet or griddle over medium-high heat. Brush lightly with margarine. Pour batter into skillet in 4-inch circles. Cook 3 to 5 minutes or until edges of pancakes are dull and bubbles form on tops. Flip pancakes; cook 1 to 2 minutes or until browned. Keep warm. Repeat with remaining batter, adding additional margarine as needed. Serve with fruit or maple syrup.

Makes about 14 pancakes

Breakfast Beans and Rice ❯

1 package (10 ounces) frozen brown rice
2 tablespoons extra virgin olive oil, divided
1 cup diced onion
1 medium poblano pepper, seeded and diced
½ (15-ounce) can black beans, rinsed and drained
1 cup diced seeded tomatoes
¼ cup chopped fresh cilantro
2 teaspoons paprika
¾ teaspoon salt
1 lime, quartered

1. Cook rice according to package directions.

2. Meanwhile, heat 1 tablespoon oil in large nonstick skillet over medium-high heat. Add onion and poblano pepper; cook and stir 4 to 5 minutes or until softened. Add beans, tomatoes, cilantro, paprika and salt; cook and stir 5 minutes.

3. Remove from heat; stir in rice and remaining 1 tablespoon oil. Squeeze lime wedge over each serving.

Makes 4 servings

Tofu, Fruit and Veggie Smoothie

1 cup frozen pineapple chunks
½ cup (4 ounces) soft tofu
½ cup apple juice
½ cup orange juice
1 container (about 2½ ounces) baby food carrots

Combine pineapple, tofu, apple juice, orange juice and carrots in blender; blend until smooth. Serve immediately.

Makes 2 servings

Satisfying Snacks

Savory Pumpkin Hummus

1 can (15 ounces) solid-pack pumpkin
3 tablespoons chopped fresh parsley, plus additional for garnish
3 tablespoons tahini
3 tablespoons fresh lemon juice
3 cloves garlic
1 teaspoon ground cumin
½ teaspoon salt
⅛ teaspoon black pepper
⅛ teaspoon ground red pepper, plus additional for garnish
Assorted cut-up vegetables

1. Combine pumpkin, 3 tablespoons parsley, tahini, lemon juice, garlic, cumin, salt, black pepper and ⅛ teaspoon ground red pepper in food processor or blender; process until smooth. Cover and refrigerate at least 2 hours to allow flavors to develop.

2. Sprinkle with additional parsley and ground red pepper, if desired. Serve with assorted vegetables.

Makes 1½ cups

Butternut Squash Oven Fries

½ teaspoon salt
½ teaspoon garlic powder
¼ teaspoon ground red pepper
**1 butternut squash (about 2½ pounds), peeled,
seeded and cut into 2-inch thin slices**
1 tablespoon vegetable oil

1. Preheat oven to 425°F. Combine salt, garlic powder and ground red pepper in small bowl.

2. Place squash on baking sheet. Drizzle with oil and sprinkle with seasoning mix; gently toss to coat. Arrange in single layer.

3. Bake 20 to 25 minutes or until squash just begins to brown, stirring frequently. *Turn oven to broil.*

4. Broil 3 to 5 minutes or until squash is browned and crisp. Spread on paper towels to cool slightly before serving.

Makes 4 servings

Spicy Roasted Chickpeas

1 can (about 15 ounces) chickpeas, rinsed and
   drained
3 tablespoons olive oil
½ teaspoon salt
½ teaspoon black pepper
¾ to 1 tablespoon chili powder
⅛ to ¼ teaspoon ground red pepper
1 lime, cut into wedges

1. Preheat oven to 400°F.

2. Combine chickpeas, oil, salt and black pepper in large bowl.
Spread in single layer on 15×10-inch jelly-roll pan.

3. Bake 15 minutes or until chickpeas begin to brown, shaking
pan twice.

4. Sprinkle with chili powder and red pepper. Bake 5 minutes
or until dark golden-red. Serve with lime wedges.

Makes 4 servings

Choco-Peanut Butter Popcorn ❯

⅓ cup semisweet chocolate chips
3 tablespoons creamy peanut butter
1 tablespoon dairy-free margarine
4 cups air-popped popcorn
½ cup powdered sugar

1. Combine chocolate chips, peanut butter and margarine in medium microwavable bowl. Microwave on HIGH 30 seconds; stir. Microwave 30 seconds or until melted and smooth.

2. Pour mixture over popcorn in large bowl, stirring until evenly coated. Transfer to 1-gallon resealable food storage bag.

3. Add powdered sugar to bag; seal bag and shake until well coated. Spread on waxed paper to cool.

Makes 6 servings

Crisp Oats Trail Mix

1 cup old-fashioned oats
½ cup unsalted shelled pumpkin seeds
½ cup dried cranberries
½ cup raisins
2 tablespoons maple syrup
1 tablespoon canola oil
½ teaspoon ground cinnamon
¼ teaspoon salt

1. Preheat oven to 325°F. Line baking sheet with heavy-duty foil. Combine all ingredients in large bowl; mix well. Spread on prepared baking sheet.

2. Bake 20 minutes or until oats are lightly browned, stirring halfway through cooking time. Cool completely on baking sheet.

Makes 2½ cups

Creamy Cashew Spread

1 cup raw cashews
2 tablespoons lemon juice
1 tablespoon tahini
½ teaspoon salt
½ teaspoon black pepper
2 teaspoons minced fresh herbs, such as basil, parsley or oregano (optional)
Melba toast and/or crackers

1. Rinse cashews and place in medium bowl. Cover with water by at least 2 inches; soak 4 hours or overnight. Drain cashews, reserving soaking water.

2. Place cashews, 2 tablespoons reserved water, lemon juice, tahini, salt and pepper in food processor or blender; process 2 to 3 minutes or until smooth. Add additional water, 1 tablespoon at a time, until desired consistency is reached. Cover and refrigerate until ready to serve.

3. Stir in herbs, if desired, just before serving. Serve with toast and/or crackers.

Makes about ½ cup

Tip:
Use as a spread or dip for hors d'oeuvres, or as a sandwich spread or pasta topping. Thin with additional liquid as needed.

Beet Chips >

3 medium beets (red and/or golden), peeled
1½ tablespoons extra virgin olive oil
½ teaspoon salt
¼ teaspoon black pepper

1. Preheat oven to 300°F.

2. Cut beets into very thin slices, about ¹⁄₁₆ inch thick. Combine beets, oil, salt and pepper in medium bowl; toss gently to coat. Arrange in single layer on baking sheets.

3. Bake 30 to 35 minutes or until darkened and crisp.* Spread on paper towels to cool completely.

If beet chips are darkened but not crisp, turn oven off and let chips stand in oven until crisp, about 10 minutes. Do not keep oven on as chips will burn easily.

Makes 2 servings

Peanutty Banana Dip

½ cup sliced banana
⅓ cup creamy peanut butter
2 tablespoons dairy-free milk
1 tablespoon agave nectar
½ teaspoon vanilla
⅛ teaspoon ground cinnamon
Sliced apples

Combine banana, peanut butter, dairy-free milk, agave, vanilla and cinnamon in blender; blend until smooth. Serve with apples for dipping.

Makes about 8 servings

Roasted Eggplant Spread

1 eggplant (1 pound)
1 medium tomato, stem removed
1 tablespoon lemon juice
1 tablespoon chopped fresh basil *or* **1 teaspoon dried basil**
2 teaspoons chopped fresh thyme *or* **¾ teaspoon dried thyme**
1 clove garlic, minced
¼ teaspoon salt
1 tablespoon extra virgin olive oil
Focaccia or pita bread wedges (optional)

1. Preheat oven to 400°F.

2. Pierce eggplant with fork in several places. Place on oven rack; roast 10 minutes. Place tomato in small baking pan; roast eggplant and tomato 40 minutes. Let stand until cool enough to handle.

3. Peel eggplant and tomato. Coarsely chop eggplant.

4. Combine, eggplant, tomato, lemon juice, basil, thyme, garlic and salt in food processor; process until well blended. With motor running, slowly add oil and process until well blended. Refrigerate 3 hours or overnight. Serve with focaccia, if desired.

Makes 10 servings

Beans and Greens Crostini

4 tablespoons olive oil, divided

1 small onion, thinly sliced

4 cups thinly sliced Italian black kale or other dinosaur kale variety

2 tablespoons minced garlic, divided

1 tablespoon balsamic vinegar

2 teaspoons salt, divided

¼ teaspoon red pepper flakes

1 can (about 15 ounces) cannellini beans, rinsed and drained

1 tablespoon chopped fresh rosemary

Toasted baguette slices

1. Heat 1 tablespoon oil in large nonstick skillet over medium heat. Add onion; cook and stir 5 minutes or until softened. Add kale and 1 tablespoon garlic; cook and stir 15 minutes or until kale is softened and most of liquid has evaporated. Stir in balsamic vinegar, 1 teaspoon salt and red pepper flakes.

2. Meanwhile, combine beans, remaining 3 tablespoons olive oil, 1 tablespoon garlic, 1 teaspoon salt and rosemary in food processor; process until smooth.

3. Spread bean mixture on baguette slices and top with kale.

Makes about 24 crostini

Almond Butter ❯

1 package (16 ounces) lightly salted roasted almonds
2 tablespoons agave nectar
1½ tablespoons canola oil

1. Grate almonds in food processor using grating disk. Remove almonds to large bowl. Replace grating disk with metal blade.

2. Transfer almonds to food processor; process 2 to 3 minutes or until nuts clump together and form thick paste, scraping side of bowl occasionally.

3. Add agave and oil; process until desired consistency is reached. Store in airtight container in refrigerator.

Makes 1½ cups

Popcorn Truffles

8 cups popped plain popcorn
2 cups (12 ounces) semisweet chocolate chips

1. Line two baking sheets with waxed paper. Place popcorn in large bowl.

2. Place chocolate chips in microwavable bowl. Microwave on HIGH 30 seconds; stir. Repeat, if necessary, until chocolate is melted. Pour over popcorn; stir until well coated.

3. Scoop popcorn mixture with small ice cream scoop, pressing mixture slightly against inside of bowl. Drop onto prepared baking sheets; allow to set at room temperature or refrigerate. Store in airtight container up to 3 days.

Makes 40 (1½-inch) truffles

Spicy Baked Sweet Potato Chips

1 teaspoon sugar
½ teaspoon salt
½ teaspoon smoked paprika
¼ teaspoon ground red pepper
2 medium sweet potatoes
4 teaspoons vegetable oil

1. Preheat oven to 400°F. Spray large baking sheet with nonstick cooking spray. Combine sugar, salt, paprika and ground red pepper in small bowl; set aside.

2. Cut sweet potatoes crosswise into very thin slices, about ¹⁄₁₆ inch thick. Place on prepared baking sheet. Drizzle with oil; toss to coat. Arrange in single layer.

3. Bake 10 minutes. Turn chips; sprinkle with seasoning mix.Bake 10 to 15 minutes or until chips are lightly browned and crisp, stirring frequently. Spread on paper towels to cool completely.

Makes 4 servings

Savory Sandwiches

Mediterranean Vegetable Sandwiches

**1 small eggplant, peeled, halved and cut into
¼-inch-thick slices**

Salt

**1 small zucchini, halved and cut lengthwise into
¼-inch-thick slices**

1 red bell pepper, cut into ¼-inch slices

2 tablespoons olive oil, divided

3 tablespoons balsamic vinegar

½ teaspoon garlic powder

2 French bread rolls, cut in half lengthwise

1. Place eggplant in non-aluminum colander; lightly sprinkle with salt. Let stand 30 minutes. Rinse eggplant; pat dry with paper towels.

2. Preheat broiler. Spray rack with nonstick cooking spray. Place vegetables on rack; brush with 1 tablespoon oil. Broil 4 inches from heat source 8 to 10 minutes or until vegetables are browned, turning once and brushing with remaining 1 tablespoon oil.

3. Whisk vinegar and garlic powder in medium bowl until well blended. Add vegetables; toss to coat. Serve immediately on rolls.

Makes 2 servings

Tempeh Melt

1 cup water
3 teaspoons hamburger seasoning
1 teaspoon paprika
**1 package (8 ounces) unseasoned soy tempeh,
  cut in half crosswise**
Thousand Island Sauce (recipe follows)
4 slices dairy-free Swiss cheese alternative
8 slices pumpernickel or marble rye bread
Dill pickle slices or sauerkraut
Red onion slices

1. Combine water, hamburger seasoning and paprika in large deep skillet. Add tempeh; bring to a boil over high heat. Reduce heat to medium-low; simmer 20 minutes, turning tempeh occasionally. Remove tempeh from skillet; cut each piece in half.

2. Meanwhile, prepare Thousand Island Sauce.

3. Prepare grill for direct cooking or preheat broiler. Grill tempeh, covered, over medium-high heat 4 minutes per side. Top with dairy-free cheese; grill 30 seconds or until cheese melts.

4. For each sandwich, spread 1 tablespoon sauce over one bread slice; top with tempeh, pickles, onions and another bread slice.

Makes 4 servings

Thousand Island Sauce: Combine ½ cup vegan mayonnaise, ½ cup chili sauce, 1 tablespoon sweet pickle relish, 2 teaspoons Dijon mustard and dash of ground red pepper in food processor; process until smooth.

Mustard Glazed Tofu Burgers

2 to 3 tablespoons chopped fresh basil

2 to 3 tablespoons honey mustard

2 teaspoons olive oil

2 cloves garlic, minced

1 package (14 ounces) extra firm tofu, pressed*

4 multigrain sandwich thin rounds, split and lightly toasted

½ cup packed arugula or watercress

8 thin slices ripe tomato

To press tofu, cut in half horizontally; cut in half crosswise to make four thin rectangles. Place tofu between layers of paper towels. Place flat, heavy object on top; let stand 15 to 30 minutes.

1. Oil grid; prepare grill for direct cooking.

2. Combine basil, mustard, oil and garlic in small bowl; mix well. Spread half of mixture over tofu.

3. Place tofu slices on grid, mustard side down; spread remaining mustard mixture over tofu. Grill, covered, 4 minutes per side or until browned and heated through.

4. Serve tofu in sandwich thins with arugula and tomato slices.

Makes 4 servings

Black Bean and Bell Pepper Wraps

2 teaspoons canola oil

1½ cups diced red, yellow and green bell peppers *or* 1 large green bell pepper, diced

½ cup chopped onion

1 can (about 15 ounces) black beans, rinsed and drained

½ cup salsa

1 teaspoon chili powder

6 (8-inch) whole wheat tortillas, warmed

¾ cup (3 ounces) shredded dairy-free cheese alternative

½ cup chopped fresh cilantro

1. Heat oil in large nonstick skillet over medium heat. Add bell peppers and onion; cook and stir 3 to 4 minutes or until softened. Stir in beans, salsa and chili powder; cook and stir 5 to 8 minutes or until vegetables are tender and sauce is thickened.

2. Spoon about ⅔ cup bean mixture down center of each tortilla. Top with dairy-free cheese and cilantro. Roll up to enclose filling.

Makes 6 servings

Ginger-Soy Grilled Tofu Sandwiches

2 tablespoons reduced-sodium soy sauce
1 tablespoon dark sesame oil
1 clove garlic, minced
1 teaspoon minced fresh ginger
¼ teaspoon red pepper flakes
1 package (14 ounces) extra firm tofu, well drained
1 large red or yellow bell pepper, cut lengthwise into quarters
1½ cups packed mixed salad greens
1 baguette (8 ounces), cut crosswise into 4 pieces and split

1. Spray grill basket, grill pan or grid with nonstick cooking spray. Prepare grill for direct cooking. Combine soy sauce, oil, garlic, ginger and red pepper flakes in small bowl; mix well. Reserve 1 tablespoon mixture in medium bowl.

2. Pat tofu dry with paper towel. Cut tofu crosswise into four thin slices; place in shallow baking dish. Spoon remaining soy sauce mixture over tofu; turn to coat.

3. Place bell pepper in grill basket; grill over medium-high heat 4 minutes. Turn bell pepper and add tofu to grill basket; grill 4 minutes. Turn bell pepper and tofu; brush tofu with any remaining soy sauce mixture from dish. Grill 3 to 4 minutes or until tofu is browned and bell pepper is tender.

4. Add salad greens to reserved soy sauce mixture; toss to coat. Serve greens, bell pepper and tofu on baguettes.

Makes 4 servings

Crunchy Vegetable Pita Pockets

2 tablespoons lime juice

2 teaspoons creamy peanut butter

2 teaspoons agave nectar

2 teaspoons soy sauce

½ teaspoon hot pepper sauce (optional)

1 cup shredded red cabbage

1 cup red bell pepper slices

½ cup frozen shelled edamame, thawed

1 whole wheat pita bread round, cut in half and lightly toasted

1. Whisk lime juice, peanut butter, agave, soy sauce and hot pepper sauce, if desired, in medium bowl until smooth and well blended. Add cabbage, bell pepper and edamame; stir to coat.

2. Serve vegetable mixture in pita bread.

Makes 2 servings

Sloppy Janes

> **2 cups TVP (textured vegetable protein)**
> **1¾ cups boiling water**
> **½ cup ketchup**
> **½ cup barbecue sauce**
> **2 tablespoons cider vinegar**
> **1 tablespoon packed brown sugar**
> **1 tablespoon soy sauce**
> **1 teaspoon chili powder**
> **1 tablespoon olive oil**
> **½ cup chopped onion**
> **½ cup chopped carrot**
> **4 to 6 hamburger or hot dog buns**

1. Combine TVP and boiling water in large bowl; let stand 10 minutes.

2. For sauce, combine ketchup, barbecue sauce, vinegar, brown sugar, soy sauce and chili powder in medium bowl.

3. Heat oil in large saucepan over medium-high heat. Add onion and carrot; cook and stir 5 minutes or until vegetables are tender. Stir in sauce mixture; bring to a boil. Stir in reconstituted TVP and ¾ cup water. Reduce heat to low; cover and cook 20 minutes. Serve mixture in buns.

Makes 4 to 6 servings

Eggless Egg Salad Sandwich

1 package (14 ounces) firm tofu, drained, pressed*
  and crumbled
1 stalk celery, finely diced
2 green onions, minced
2 tablespoons minced parsley
¼ cup plus 1 tablespoon vegan mayonnaise
3 tablespoons sweet pickle relish
2 teaspoons lemon juice
1 teaspoon mustard
  Black pepper
8 slices whole wheat bread, toasted
1½ cups alfalfa sprouts
8 tomato slices

*To press tofu, cut in half horizontally and place between layers of paper towels.
Place flat, heavy object on top; let stand 15 to 30 minutes.

1. Combine tofu, celery, green onions and parsley in large bowl.
Stir mayonnaise, relish, lemon juice, mustard and pepper in small
bowl until well blended. Add to tofu mixture; mix well.

2. Serve salad on toast with alfalfa sprouts and tomato slices.

Makes 4 sandwiches

Grilled Vegetable and Hummus Muffaletta

1 small eggplant, cut lengthwise into ⅛-inch slices
1 yellow squash, cut lengthwise into ⅛-inch slices
1 zucchini, cut on the diagonal into ⅛-inch slices
¼ cup extra virgin olive oil
½ teaspoon salt
¼ teaspoon black pepper
1 (8-inch) boule or round bread, cut in half horizontally
1 container (8 ounces) hummus, any flavor
1 jar (12 ounces) roasted red bell peppers, drained
1 jar (6 ounces) marinated artichoke hearts, drained and chopped
1 small tomato, thinly sliced

1. Preheat grill or grill pan. Combine eggplant, squash, zucchini, oil, salt and pepper in large bowl; toss to coat. Grill vegetables 2 to 3 minutes per side or until tender and golden brown. Cool to room temperature.

2. Scoop out bread from both halves of bread, leaving about 1 inch of bread on edges and about 1½ inches on bottom. (Reserve bread for bread crumbs or croutons.)

3. Spread hummus evenly on bottom half of bread. Layer grilled vegetables, roasted peppers, artichokes and tomato over hummus; cover with top half of bread. Wrap sandwich tightly with plastic wrap. Refrigerate at least 1 hour before cutting into wedges.

Makes 6 servings

Pasta Pronto

Summer Spaghetti

1 pound plum tomatoes, coarsely chopped
1 small onion, chopped
6 pitted green olives, chopped
⅓ cup chopped fresh parsley
2 tablespoons finely shredded fresh basil
   ***or* ¾ teaspoon dried basil**
2 cloves garlic, minced
2 teaspoons drained capers
½ teaspoon paprika
¼ teaspoon dried oregano
½ cup olive oil
1 tablespoon red wine vinegar
1 pound uncooked spaghetti

1. Combine tomatoes, onion, olives, parsley, basil, garlic, capers, paprika and oregano in medium bowl; mix well. Stir in oil and vinegar.

2. Cook pasta according to package directions; drain. Toss hot pasta with tomato mixture. Serve immediately.

Makes 4 to 6 servings

Tip: The tomato mixture can be made up to one day in advance. Cover and refrigerate until ready to use.

Curried Noodles

7 ounces thin rice noodles (rice vermicelli)
1 tablespoon peanut or vegetable oil
1 large red bell pepper, cut into short, thin strips
2 green onions, cut into ½-inch pieces
1 clove garlic, minced
1 teaspoon minced fresh ginger
2 teaspoons curry powder
⅛ to ¼ teaspoon red pepper flakes
½ cup vegetable broth
2 tablespoons soy sauce

1. Place noodles in large bowl; cover with boiling water. Let stand 15 minutes to soften. Drain and cut into 3-inch pieces.

2. Heat oil in wok or large skillet over medium-high heat. Add bell pepper; stir-fry 3 minutes.

3. Add green onions, garlic and ginger; stir-fry 1 minute. Add curry powder and red pepper flakes; stir-fry 1 minute.

4. Add broth and soy sauce; cook and stir 2 minutes. Add noodles; cook and stir 3 minutes or until heated through.

Makes 6 servings

Penne Pasta with Chunky Tomato Sauce and Spinach

8 ounces multigrain penne pasta

2 cups spicy marinara sauce

1 large ripe tomato, chopped (about 1½ cups)

4 cups packed baby spinach or torn spinach leaves (4 ounces)

¼ cup vegan Parmesan-flavor topping

¼ cup chopped fresh basil

1. Cook pasta according to package directions.

2. Meanwhile, heat marinara sauce and tomato in medium saucepan over medium heat 3 to 4 minutes or until hot and bubbly, stirring occasionally. Remove from heat; stir in spinach.

3. Drain pasta; return to saucepan. Add sauce; toss to coat. Divide evenly among serving bowls; top with Parmesan-flavor topping and basil.

Makes 4 to 6 servings

Spicy Sesame Noodles

6 ounces uncooked soba (buckwheat) noodles
2 teaspoons dark sesame oil
1 tablespoon sesame seeds
½ cup vegetable broth
1 tablespoon creamy peanut butter
½ cup thinly sliced green onions
½ cup minced red bell pepper
4 teaspoons reduced-sodium soy sauce
1½ teaspoons finely chopped seeded jalapeño pepper*
1 clove garlic, minced
¼ teaspoon red pepper flakes

*Jalapeño peppers can sting and irritate the skin, so wear rubber gloves when handling peppers and do not touch your eyes.

1. Cook noodles according to package directions. *Do not overcook.* Rinse noodles thoroughly under cold running water; drain. Place in large bowl; toss with oil.

2. Cook sesame seeds in small skillet over medium heat about 3 minutes or until seeds begin to pop and turn golden brown, stirring frequently. Remove from skillet.

3. Whisk broth and peanut butter in medium bowl until blended. (Mixture may look curdled.) Stir in green onions, bell pepper, soy sauce, jalapeño, garlic and red pepper flakes.

4. Pour mixture over noodles; toss to coat. Cover and let stand 30 minutes at room temperature or refrigerate up to 24 hours. Sprinkle with toasted sesame seeds before serving.

Makes 6 servings

Rigatoni Salad

12 ounces uncooked rigatoni pasta

1 to 2 cups chopped greens, such as arugula, frisée or any crisp lettuce

1 package (10 ounces) frozen snow peas or sugar snap peas, thawed

8 ounces cherry tomatoes, cut into halves

1 medium red or yellow bell pepper, cut into thin strips

½ red onion, cut into thin strips

⅓ cup sliced black olives

⅓ to ½ cup Italian salad dressing

Vegan Parmesan-flavor topping (optional)

1. Cook pasta according to package directions; drain and rinse under cool water.

2. Combine pasta, greens, snow peas, tomatoes, bell pepper, onion and olives in large bowl. Add dressing; toss gently to coat. Sprinkle with Parmesan-flavor topping, if desired.

Makes about 8 servings

Tip:

Vary the amounts of each ingredient according to your taste. Substitute steamed green beans (whole or cut) for the peas or add steamed sliced carrots, zucchini or yellow squash.

Tofu and Snow Pea Noodle Bowl

5 cups water

6 tablespoons chicken-flavored broth powder*

4 ounces uncooked vermicelli, broken in thirds

½ pound firm tofu, rinsed, patted dry and cut into
¼-inch cubes

1 cup (3 ounces) fresh snow peas

1 cup matchstick-size carrot strips

½ teaspoon chili garlic sauce

½ cup chopped green onions

¼ cup chopped fresh cilantro (optional)

2 tablespoons lime juice

1 tablespoon grated fresh ginger

2 teaspoons soy sauce

Chicken-flavored vegetarian broth powder can be found in natural food stores and some supermarkets. If broth powder is unavailable, substitute 5 cups vegetable broth for the water and broth powder.

1. Bring water to a boil in large saucepan over high heat. Stir in broth powder and pasta; return to a boil. Reduce heat to medium; simmer 6 minutes. Stir in tofu, snow peas, carrots and chili garlic sauce; simmer 2 minutes.

2. Remove from heat; stir in green onions, cilantro, if desired, lime juice, ginger and soy sauce. Serve immediately.

Makes 4 servings

Quick Szechuan Vegetable Lo Mein

2 cans (about 14 ounces each) vegetable broth
2 teaspoons minced garlic
1 teaspoon minced fresh ginger
¼ teaspoon red pepper flakes
1 package (16 ounces) frozen vegetable medley, such as broccoli, carrots, water chestnuts and red bell peppers
1 package (5 ounces) Asian curly noodles or 5 ounces uncooked angel hair pasta, broken in half
3 tablespoons soy sauce
1 tablespoon dark sesame oil
¼ cup thinly sliced green onions

1. Combine broth, garlic, ginger and red pepper flakes in wok or deep skillet; bring to a boil over high heat. Add vegetables and noodles; cover and return to a boil. Reduce heat to medium-low; simmer, uncovered, 5 to 6 minutes or until vegetables and noodles are tender, stirring occasionally.

2. Stir in soy sauce and sesame oil; cook 3 minutes. Stir in green onions just before serving.

Makes 4 servings

Note: For a heartier, protein-packed main dish, add 1 package (14 ounces) extra firm tofu, drained and cut into ¾-inch cubes, to the broth mixture with the soy sauce and sesame oil.

Lemon-Tossed Linguine

8 ounces uncooked linguine
3 tablespoons fresh lemon juice
2 teaspoons dairy-free margarine
2 tablespoons minced chives
⅓ cup dairy-free milk
1 teaspoon cornstarch
1 tablespoon minced fresh dill
1 tablespoon minced fresh parsley
2 teaspoons grated lemon peel
¼ teaspoon white pepper
3 tablespoons vegan Parmesan-flavor topping

1. Cook pasta according to package directions; drain well. Place in medium bowl; sprinkle with lemon juice.

2. Meanwhile, melt margarine in small saucepan over medium heat. Add chives; cook and stir until softened.

3. Stir dairy-free milk into cornstarch in small bowl until smooth. Add to saucepan; cook and stir until thickened. Stir in dill, parsley, lemon peel and pepper.

4. Pour sauce over noodles. Sprinkle with Parmesan-flavor topping; toss to coat. Garnish, if desired. Serve immediately.

Makes 2 servings

Peanut-Sauced Pasta

⅓ cup vegetable broth
3 tablespoons creamy peanut butter
2 tablespoons seasoned rice vinegar
2 tablespoons reduced-sodium soy sauce
½ teaspoon red pepper flakes
9 ounces uncooked multigrain linguine
1½ pounds fresh asparagus, cut into 1-inch pieces
　　(4 cups)
⅓ cup dry-roasted peanuts, chopped

1. Whisk broth, peanut butter, vinegar, soy sauce and red pepper flakes in small saucepan until smooth. Cook over low heat until heated through, stirring frequently. Keep warm.

2. Cook pasta according to package directions. Add asparagus to saucepan during last 5 minutes of cooking. Drain pasta and asparagus; toss with peanut sauce. Sprinkle with peanuts.

Makes 4 servings

Fast Favorites

Spanish Rice with Chorizo

1 tablespoon olive oil
12 ounces soy chorizo, casings removed, sliced
1 green bell pepper, diced
2 cloves garlic, minced
½ teaspoon smoked paprika
1½ cups uncooked instant rice
1 can (about 14 ounces) diced tomatoes
1 cup vegetable broth or water
2 green onions, chopped
Salt and black pepper

1. Heat oil in large nonstick skillet over medium heat. Add soy chorizo, bell pepper, garlic and paprika; cook and stir 5 minutes or until bell pepper is tender. Stir in rice, tomatoes, broth and green onions; bring to a boil over high heat.

2. Reduce heat to medium-low; cover and simmer 8 to 10 minutes or until liquid is absorbed and rice is tender. Season with salt and black pepper.

Makes 4 servings

Tex-Mex Black Bean and Corn Stew

1 tablespoon canola or vegetable oil

1 small onion, chopped

4 cloves garlic, minced

1 teaspoon chili powder

1 teaspoon ground cumin

1 can (about 15 ounces) black beans, rinsed and drained

1 can (about 14 ounces) fire-roasted diced tomatoes

2 medium zucchini or yellow squash (or one of each), cut into ½-inch pieces

1 cup frozen corn

¾ cup salsa

½ cup (2 ounces) shredded dairy-free cheese alternative

¼ cup finely chopped fresh cilantro or green onion

1. Heat oil in large saucepan over medium heat. Add onion; cook and stir 5 minutes. Add garlic, chili powder and cumin; cook and stir 1 minute.

2. Stir in beans, tomatoes, zucchini, corn and salsa, bring to a boil over high heat. Reduce heat to medium-low; cover and simmer 20 minutes or until vegetables are tender.

3. Ladle into bowls; top with dairy-free cheese and cilantro.

Makes 4 servings

Roasted Sweet Potato and Apple Salad

2 large sweet potatoes, peeled and cubed
2 tablespoons olive oil, divided
¾ teaspoon salt, divided
¼ teaspoon black pepper
3 tablespoons apple juice
1 tablespoon Dijon mustard
1 tablespoon agave nectar
1 tablespoon balsamic vinegar
2 teaspoons snipped fresh chives
1 medium Gala apple, chopped (about 1 cup)
½ cup finely chopped celery
¼ cup thinly sliced red onion
    Lettuce leaves (optional)

1. Preheat oven to 450°F. Place sweet potatoes on large baking sheet. Drizzle with 1 tablespoon oil and sprinkle with ½ teaspoon salt and pepper; toss to coat. Spread in single layer.

2. Roast 20 to 25 minutes or until sweet potatoes are tender, stirring halfway through baking. Cool completely.

3. Meanwhile, whisk apple juice, remaining 1 tablespoon oil, mustard, agave, vinegar, chives and remaining ¼ teaspoon salt in small bowl until well blended.

4. Combine sweet potatoes, apple, celery and onion in medium bowl. Drizzle with dressing; gently toss to coat. Serve over lettuce leaves, if desired.

Makes 4 servings

Couscous with Carrots and Cranberries

2 cups vegetable broth
2 teaspoons olive oil
½ onion, thinly sliced
½ carrot, grated using large holes of box grater
¼ cup dried cranberries, chopped
¼ teaspoon ground cinnamon
¼ teaspoon ground cumin
¼ teaspoon ground turmeric
1 cup whole wheat couscous
    Salt and black pepper

1. Bring broth to a boil in medium saucepan over medium heat.

2. Meanwhile, heat oil in small saucepan over medium-low heat. Add onion; cook and stir 2 minutes or until translucent. Add carrot; cook and stir 1 minute. Add cranberries; cook 30 seconds.

3. Add cinnamon, cumin and turmeric; mix well. Cook 15 to 20 seconds or until fragrant. Stir in couscous until well blended.

4. Stir couscous mixture into broth; remove from heat. Season with salt and pepper. Cover and let stand 10 to 15 minutes or until couscous is tender. Fluff couscous just before serving.

Makes 4 servings

Miso Soup with Tofu

4 cups water
1 tablespoon shredded nori or wakame seaweed
8 ounces firm tofu
3 green onions, finely chopped
¼ cup white miso
2 teaspoons soy sauce

1. Bring water to a simmer in medium saucepan over medium-low heat. Add nori; simmer 6 minutes.

2. Meanwhile, press tofu between paper towels to remove excess water. Cut into ½-inch cubes.

3. Reduce heat to low. Add tofu, green onions, miso and soy sauce; cook and stir until miso is dissolved and soup is heated through. *Do not boil.*

Makes 4 servings

Chunky Black Bean and Sweet Potato Chili

2 teaspoons vegetable oil

1 cup chopped sweet onion

2 red or green bell peppers (or one of each), cut into ½-inch pieces

4 cloves garlic, minced

1 teaspoon chili powder

1 can (about 14 ounces) fire-roasted diced tomatoes

1 small sweet potato (8 ounces), peeled and cut into ½-inch pieces (1½ cups)

1 tablespoon minced chipotle chiles in adobo sauce

1 can (about 15 ounces) black beans, rinsed and drained

½ cup chopped cilantro (optional)

1. Heat oil in large saucepan over medium heat. Add onion; cook and stir 5 minutes. Add bell peppers, garlic and chili powder; cook and stir 2 minutes. Add tomatoes, sweet potato and chipotle; bring to a boil. Reduce heat to medium-low; cover and simmer 15 minutes.

2. Stir in beans; cover and simmer 8 to 10 minutes or until vegetables are tender. (Chili will be thick; thin with water if desired.)

3. Ladle chili into bowls; top with cilantro, if desired.

Makes about 4 servings

Quinoa and Mango Salad

1 cup uncooked quinoa
2 cups water
2 cups cubed peeled mango (about 2 large mangoes)
½ cup sliced green onions
½ cup dried cranberries
2 tablespoons chopped fresh parsley
¼ cup extra virgin olive oil
1½ tablespoons white wine vinegar
1 teaspoon Dijon mustard
½ teaspoon salt
⅛ teaspoon black pepper

1. Place quinoa in fine-mesh strainer; rinse well under cold running water. Bring 2 cups water to a boil in small saucepan over high heat; stir in quinoa. Reduce heat to low; cover and simmer 10 to 15 minutes until quinoa is tender and water is absorbed. Stir quinoa; let stand, covered, 15 minutes. Transfer to large bowl; cover and refrigerate at least 1 hour.

2. Add mangoes, green onions, cranberries and parsley to quinoa; mix well.

3. Combine oil, vinegar, mustard, salt and pepper in small bowl; whisk until blended. Pour over quinoa mixture; mix well.

Makes 8 servings

Tip: This salad can be made several hours ahead and refrigerated. Let it stand at room temperature for at least 30 minutes before serving.

Sweet Onion and Pumpkin Seed Focaccia

1 package (about 14 ounces) refrigerated pizza dough
¼ cup olive oil
2 red onions, thinly sliced
¼ cup unsalted shelled pumpkin seeds
½ teaspoon dried oregano
¼ teaspoon salt
⅛ teaspoon red pepper flakes
⅛ teaspoon black pepper

1. Preheat oven to 400°F. Spray jelly-roll pan with nonstick cooking spray or line with parchment paper.

2. Unroll dough on prepared baking sheet; press into 15×10-inch rectangle. Bake 10 minutes.

3. Meanwhile, heat oil in large skillet over medium-high heat. Add onions; cook and stir 7 minutes or until just tender. Add pumpkin seeds, oregano, salt, red pepper flakes and black pepper; cook and stir 3 minutes.

4. Remove crust from oven. Spread onion mixture evenly over crust. Bake 10 to 14 minutes or until crust is golden and onions begin to brown. Let stand 5 minutes before cutting.

Makes 10 servings

Tofu "Fried" Rice

2 ounces extra firm tofu
¼ cup finely chopped broccoli
¼ cup thawed frozen shelled edamame
⅓ cup cooked brown rice
1 tablespoon chopped green onion
½ teaspoon reduced-sodium soy sauce
¼ teaspoon sesame oil
⅛ teaspoon garlic powder
⅛ teaspoon sriracha* or hot chili sauce (optional)

*Sriracha is a Thai hot sauce that can be found in the Asian section or the condiment aisle of major supermarkets.

1. Press tofu between paper towels to remove excess water. Cut into ½-inch cubes.

2. Combine tofu, broccoli and edamame in large microwavable mug or bowl.

3. Microwave on HIGH 1 minute. Stir in rice, green onion, soy sauce, oil, garlic powder and sriracha, if desired. Microwave 1 minute or until heated through. Stir before serving.

Makes 1 serving

Couscous and Black Bean Salad

1⅓ cups cooked whole wheat couscous
1 can (about 15 ounces) black beans, rinsed and
   drained
1 cup cherry tomatoes
2 tablespoons minced fresh chives or green onion
1 tablespoon minced fresh cilantro
1 small jalapeño pepper,* seeded and minced
   (optional)
1 tablespoon olive oil
2 teaspoons white wine vinegar
½ teaspoon salt
⅛ teaspoon black pepper

*Jalapeño peppers can sting and irritate the skin, so wear rubber gloves when handling peppers and do not touch your eyes.

1. Combine couscous and beans in large bowl. Cut tomatoes in half, reserving 1 tablespoon tomato juice. Add tomatoes to couscous mixture. Stir in chives, cilantro and jalapeño pepper, if desired; mix gently.

2. Whisk oil, vinegar, reserved tomato juice, salt and black pepper in small bowl until well blended. Pour over salad; toss to coat.

Makes 4 servings

Kale, Mushroom and Caramelized Onion Pizza

1 package (about 14 ounces) refrigerated pizza dough
1 tablespoon olive oil
1 cup chopped yellow onion
1 package (8 ounces) sliced mushrooms
3 cloves garlic, minced
4 cups packed coarsely chopped kale
¼ teaspoon red pepper flakes
½ cup dairy-free pizza sauce
¾ cup (3 ounces) shredded dairy-free mozzarella cheese alternative

1. Preheat oven to 425°F. Spray 15×10-inch jelly-roll pan with nonstick cooking spray or line with parchment paper.

2. Unroll dough on prepared pan; press evenly into pan and ½ inch up sides. Prick dough all over with fork. Bake 7 to 10 minutes or until lightly browned.

3. Meanwhile, heat oil in large nonstick skillet over medium heat. Add onion; cook and stir 8 minutes or until golden brown. Add mushrooms and garlic; cook and stir 4 minutes. Add kale and red pepper flakes; cover and cook 2 minutes to wilt kale. Uncover; cook and stir 3 to 4 minutes or until vegetables are tender.

4. Spread pizza sauce over crust. Spread kale mixture evenly over sauce; top with dairy-free mozzarella. Bake 10 minutes or until crust is golden brown.

Makes 4 servings

Fruit and Nut Quinoa

1 cup uncooked quinoa
2 cups water
2 tablespoons finely grated orange peel
¼ cup fresh orange juice
2 teaspoons olive oil
½ teaspoon salt
¼ teaspoon ground cinnamon
⅓ cup dried cranberries
⅓ cup toasted shelled pistachio nuts*

To toast pistachios, spread in single layer in heavy skillet. Cook over medium heat 1 to 2 minutes or until nuts are lightly browned, stirring frequently.

1. Place quinoa in fine-mesh strainer; rinse well under cold running water. Bring 2 cups water to a boil in small saucepan over high heat; stir in quinoa. Reduce heat to low; cover and simmer 10 to 15 minutes or until quinoa is tender and water is absorbed. Stir in orange peel.

2. Whisk orange juice, oil, salt and cinnamon in small bowl until well blended. Pour over quinoa; toss gently to coat. Fold in cranberries and pistachios. Serve warm or at room temperature.

Makes 6 servings

Table of Contents

Hearty Bowls

Mushroom Barley Stew

1 tablespoon olive oil
1 medium onion, finely chopped
1 cup chopped carrots (about 2 carrots)
1 clove garlic, minced
5 cups vegetable broth
1 cup uncooked pearl barley
1 cup chopped dried mushrooms
1 teaspoon salt
½ teaspoon dried thyme
½ teaspoon black pepper

Slow Cooker Directions

1. Heat oil in medium skillet over medium-high heat. Add onion, carrots and garlic; cook and stir 5 minutes or until tender. Transfer to slow cooker.

2. Add broth, barley, mushrooms, salt, thyme and pepper to slow cooker; mix well. Cover; cook on LOW 6 to 7 hours.

Makes 4 to 6 servings

Variation: To turn this thick, robust stew into a soup, add 2 to 3 additional cups of broth. Cook as directed above.

Lentil Chili

1 tablespoon canola oil
4 cloves garlic, minced
1 tablespoon chili powder
4 cups vegetable broth
¾ cup dried brown or green lentils, rinsed and sorted
2 teaspoons smoked chipotle hot pepper sauce
2 cups diced peeled butternut squash
1 can (about 14 ounces) diced tomatoes
½ cup chopped fresh cilantro
¼ cup shelled pumpkin seeds (optional)

1. Heat oil in large saucepan over medium heat. Add garlic; cook and stir 1 minute. Add chili powder; cook and stir 30 seconds.

2. Add broth, lentils and hot pepper sauce; bring to a boil over high heat. Reduce heat to low; simmer 15 minutes. Stir in squash and tomatoes; simmer 18 to 20 minutes or until lentils and squash are tender.

3. Top with cilantro and pumpkin seeds, if desired.

Makes 4 servings

Caribbean Sweet Potato and Bean Stew

2 medium sweet potatoes (about 1 pound), peeled and cut into 1-inch cubes

2 cups frozen cut green beans

1 can (about 15 ounces) black beans, rinsed and drained

1 can (about 14 ounces) vegetable broth

1 small onion, sliced

2 teaspoons Caribbean jerk seasoning

½ teaspoon dried thyme

¼ teaspoon salt

¼ teaspoon ground cinnamon

⅓ cup slivered almonds, toasted*

Hot pepper sauce (optional)

*To toast almonds, spread in single layer on baking sheet. Bake in preheated 350°F oven 8 to 10 minutes or until golden brown, stirring frequently.

Slow Cooker Directions

1. Combine sweet potatoes, green beans, black beans, broth, onion, seasoning, thyme, salt and cinnamon in slow cooker. Cover; cook on LOW 5 to 6 hours or until vegetables are tender.

2. Top with almonds; serve with hot pepper sauce, if desired.

Makes 4 servings

Middle Eastern Vegetable Stew

¼ cup olive oil

3 cups (12 ounces) sliced zucchini

2 cups (6 ounces) cubed peeled eggplant

2 cups peeled, quartered and sliced sweet potatoes

1½ cups cubed peeled butternut squash (optional)

1 can (28 ounces) crushed tomatoes in purée

1 cup drained canned chickpeas

½ cup raisins or currants (optional)

1½ teaspoons ground cinnamon

1 teaspoon grated orange peel

¾ teaspoon ground cumin

½ teaspoon salt

½ teaspoon paprika

¼ to ½ teaspoon ground red pepper

⅛ teaspoon ground cardamom

Hot cooked whole wheat couscous or brown rice (optional)

1. Heat oil in large saucepan or Dutch oven over medium heat. Add zucchini, eggplant, sweet potatoes and squash, if desired; cook and stir 8 to 10 minutes until vegetables are slightly softened.

2. Add tomatoes, chickpeas, raisins, if desired, cinnamon, orange peel, cumin, salt, paprika, ground red pepper and cardamom; bring to a boil over high heat.

3. Reduce heat to low; cover and simmer 30 minutes or until vegetables are tender. If sauce becomes too thick, add water to thin. Serve over couscous, if desired.

Makes 6 servings

Black Bean Chili

1 pound uncooked dried black beans, rinsed and sorted

Cold water

6 cups water

1 bay leaf

3 tablespoons vegetable oil

2 large onions, chopped

3 cloves garlic, minced

1 can (about 14 ounces) diced tomatoes

2 jalapeño peppers,* seeded and minced

2 tablespoons chili powder

1½ teaspoons salt

1 teaspoon paprika

1 teaspoon dried oregano

1 teaspoon unsweetened cocoa powder

½ teaspoon ground cumin

¼ teaspoon ground cinnamon

1 tablespoon red wine vinegar

Picante sauce (optional)

½ cup sliced green onions and/or chopped fresh cilantro (optional)

Jalapeño peppers can sting and irritate the skin, so wear rubber gloves when handling peppers and do not touch your eyes.

1. Place beans in Dutch oven; add cold water to cover by 2 inches. Cover and bring to a boil over high heat. Boil 2 minutes. Remove from heat; let stand, covered, 1 hour. Drain water; return beans to Dutch oven.

2. Add 6 cups water and bay leaf to beans in Dutch oven; bring to a boil over high heat. Reduce heat to low; simmer, partially covered, 1 to 2 hours or until beans are tender.

3. Meanwhile, heat oil in large skillet over medium heat. Add onions and garlic; cook about 6 minutes or until onions are tender. Add tomatoes, jalapeños, chili powder, salt, paprika, oregano, cocoa, cumin and cinnamon; simmer 15 minutes.

4. Add tomato mixture and vinegar to beans; mix well. Simmer 30 minutes or until beans are very tender and chili has thickened slightly. Remove and discard bay leaf. Serve with desired toppings.

Makes 6 servings

Italian Escarole and White Bean Stew

1 tablespoon olive oil
1 onion, chopped
3 carrots, cut into ½-inch-thick rounds
2 cloves garlic, minced
1 can (about 14 ounces) vegetable broth
1 head escarole (about 12 ounces)
¼ teaspoon red pepper flakes
2 cans (about 15 ounces each) Great Northern
    beans, rinsed and drained
Salt
Vegan Parmesan-flavor topping (optional)

Slow Cooker Directions

1. Heat oil in medium skillet over medium-high heat. Add onion and carrots; cook and stir about 5 minutes or until onion is softened. Add garlic; cook and stir 1 minute. Transfer to slow cooker. Pour in broth.

2. Trim base of escarole. Roughly cut leaves crosswise into 1-inch-wide strips. Wash well in large bowl of cold water. Lift out by handfuls, leaving sand or dirt in bottom of bowl. Shake to remove excess water, but do not dry. Add to slow cooker. Sprinkle with red pepper flakes; top with beans.

3. Cover; cook on LOW 7 to 8 hours or on HIGH 3½ to 4 hours or until escarole is wilted and very tender. Season with salt. Sprinkle with Parmesan-flavor topping, if desired.

Makes 4 servings

Tip: Escarole is very leafy and easily fills a 4½-quart slow cooker when raw, but it shrinks dramatically as it cooks down.

Four-Bean Chili

　　　2 tablespoons vegetable oil
　　　1 onion, coarsely chopped
　　　3 cloves garlic, minced
　　　1 zucchini, halved lengthwise and thinly sliced
　　　½ red bell pepper, chopped
　　　2 cans (11 ounces each) tomatillos, drained
　　　1 can (about 15 ounces) red kidney beans, rinsed and drained
　　　1 can (about 15 ounces) black beans, rinsed and drained
　　　1 can (about 15 ounces) Great Northern beans, rinsed and drained
　　　1 can (about 15 ounces) chickpeas, rinsed and drained
　　　1 can (15 ounces) tomato sauce
　　　½ cup barbecue sauce
　　1½ teaspoons ground cumin
　　　1 to 1½ teaspoons chili powder
　　　½ teaspoon salt
　　　¼ to ½ teaspoon ground red pepper
　　　　Chopped tomato, chopped onion and/or chopped fresh cilantro (optional)

1. Heat oil in Dutch oven over medium-high heat. Add onion and garlic; cook and stir until onion is soft. Add zucchini and bell pepper; cook and stir 5 minutes.

2. Add tomatillos, beans, chickpeas, tomato sauce, barbecue sauce, cumin, chili powder, salt and ground red pepper; bring to a boil over high heat. Reduce heat to low; cover and simmer 30 minutes.

3. Serve chili with desired toppings.

Makes 4 to 6 servings

Lentil and Spinach Stew

1 tablespoon olive oil
3 medium stalks celery, cut into ½-inch pieces
3 medium carrots, cut into ½-inch pieces
1 medium onion, chopped
3 cloves garlic, minced
4 cups vegetable broth
1 can (about 14 ounces) diced tomatoes
1 cup dried brown lentils, rinsed and sorted
2 teaspoons ground cumin
½ teaspoon dried basil
½ teaspoon salt
¼ teaspoon black pepper
5 cups baby spinach
3 cups hot cooked ditalini pasta

Slow Cooker Directions

1. Heat oil in large skillet over medium-high heat. Add celery, carrots, onion and garlic; cook and stir 3 to 4 minutes or until vegetables begin to soften.

2. Spray slow cooker with nonstick cooking spray. Transfer vegetable mixture to slow cooker. Stir in broth, tomatoes, lentils, cumin, basil, salt and pepper. Cover; cook on LOW 8 to 9 hours or until lentils are tender but still hold their shape.

3. Stir in spinach just before serving. Serve over pasta.

Makes 4 servings

Chickpea Vegetable Soup

1 tablespoon olive oil

1 cup chopped onion

½ cup chopped green bell pepper

2 cloves garlic, minced

2 cans (about 14 ounces each) diced tomatoes

3 cups water

2 cups broccoli florets

1 can (about 15 ounces) chickpeas, rinsed, drained and slightly mashed

½ cup (3 ounces) uncooked orzo or rosamarina pasta

1 whole bay leaf

1 tablespoon chopped fresh thyme *or* 1 teaspoon dried thyme

1 tablespoon chopped fresh rosemary leaves *or* 1 teaspoon dried rosemary

1 tablespoon lime or lemon juice

½ teaspoon ground turmeric

¼ teaspoon salt

¼ teaspoon ground red pepper

¼ cup pumpkin seeds or sunflower kernels (optional)

1. Heat oil in large saucepan over medium heat. Add onion, bell pepper and garlic; cook and stir 5 minutes or until vegetables are tender.

2. Add tomatoes, water, broccoli, chickpeas, pasta, bay leaf, thyme, rosemary, lime juice, turmeric, salt and red pepper; bring to a boil over high heat. Reduce heat to medium-low; cover and simmer 10 to 12 minutes or until pasta is tender.

3. Remove and discard bay leaf. Sprinkle with pumpkin seeds, if desired.

Makes 4 servings

Lotsa Pasta

Vegan Pesto

1 pound uncooked whole wheat fettuccine
1 cup packed fresh basil leaves
½ cup pine nuts, toasted*
2 cloves garlic
½ teaspoon salt
¼ teaspoon black pepper
¼ cup plus 1 tablespoon olive oil, divided

*To toast pine nuts, spread in single layer in small skillet. Cook over low heat 2 minutes or until light brown and fragrant, shaking occasionally.

1. Cook pasta according to package directions; drain and keep warm.

2. Meanwhile, combine basil, pine nuts, garlic, salt and pepper in food processor; drizzle with 1 tablespoon olive oil. Process about 10 seconds or until coarsely chopped. With motor running, drizzle in remaining ¼ cup olive oil. Process about 30 seconds or until almost smooth. Toss with hot cooked pasta.

Makes 4 servings

Note: Pesto can be made 1 week in advance. Transfer to covered container and store in refrigerator. Makes ½ cup pesto.

Whole Wheat Penne with Vegetables

6 ounces uncooked whole wheat penne pasta (about 2 cups)

1 tablespoon olive oil

1½ cups chopped fresh broccoli

1 medium zucchini, chopped

½ medium yellow bell pepper, chopped

2 cloves garlic, minced

8 ounces cherry or grape tomatoes, halved (about 1½ cups)

4 ounces mushrooms, sliced (about 1 cup)

½ teaspoon dried oregano

¾ cup crumbled dairy-free feta cheese*

*Use purchased dairy-free feta cheese or prepare Dairy-Free Feta (page 182).

1. Cook pasta according to package directions; drain and keep warm.

2. Heat oil in large nonstick skillet over medium-high heat. Add broccoli, zucchini, bell pepper and garlic; cook and stir about 2 minutes or until vegetables just begin to soften.

3. Add tomatoes, mushrooms and oregano; cook and stir over medium heat about 8 minutes or until vegetables are tender and tomatoes release their juices.

4. Combine vegetables and pasta in large bowl. Add dairy-free feta; toss gently.

Makes 4 servings

Vegan Artichoke Lasagna

1 tablespoon olive oil

1 cup chopped onion

3 cloves garlic, minced

¼ cup tomato paste

¼ cup white wine

1 can (28 ounces) Italian plum tomatoes, undrained, or crushed tomatoes

1 teaspoon coarse salt

1 teaspoon sugar

1 teaspoon dried oregano

9 uncooked lasagna noodles

Not-Ricotta (page 127)

1 can (14 ounces) artichoke hearts, drained and chopped

1 package (10 ounces) frozen chopped spinach, thawed and squeezed dry

2 cups (8 ounces) shredded dairy-free mozzarella cheese alternative

2 roasted bell peppers, chopped

1. For sauce, heat oil in large saucepan over medium-high heat. Add onion and garlic; cook and stir 5 minutes or until onion is tender. Stir in tomato paste; cook 1 minute. Stir in wine; cook 30 seconds. Add tomatoes with juice, salt, sugar and oregano; break up tomatoes with spoon. Reduce heat to low; cover and simmer 30 minutes.

2. Meanwhile, cook lasagna noodles according to package directions; drain and return to saucepan. Cover with cold water to prevent sticking.

3. Prepare Not-Ricotta. Combine artichokes and spinach in medium bowl.

4. Preheat oven to 350°F. Spray 13×9-inch baking dish with nonstick cooking spray. Spread ½ cup sauce in dish; arrange three noodles over sauce. Spread half of Not-Ricotta over noodles; top with artichoke mixture, half of shredded dairy-free mozzarella and ½ cup sauce. Repeat layers of noodles and Not-Ricotta; top with roasted peppers, remaining three noodles, sauce and dairy-free mozzarella.

5. Cover with greased foil; bake 45 minutes. Remove foil; bake 15 minutes. Let stand 10 minutes before serving.

Makes 8 servings

Vegetarian Rice Noodles

½ cup soy sauce

⅓ cup sugar

¼ cup lime juice

2 fresh red Thai chiles *or* 1 large jalapeño pepper,*
finely chopped

8 ounces thin rice noodles (rice vermicelli)

¼ cup vegetable oil

8 ounces firm tofu, drained and cut into triangles

1 jicama (8 ounces), peeled and chopped *or* 1 can
(8 ounces) sliced water chestnuts, drained

2 medium sweet potatoes (1 pound), peeled and cut
into ¼-inch-thick slices

2 large leeks, cut crosswise into ¼-inch-thick slices

¼ cup chopped dry-roasted peanuts

2 tablespoons chopped fresh mint

2 tablespoons chopped fresh cilantro

Chile peppers can sting and irritate the skin, so wear rubber gloves when handling peppers and do not touch your eyes.

1. Combine soy sauce, sugar, lime juice and chiles in small bowl until well blended; set aside.

2. Place rice noodles in medium bowl. Cover with hot water; let stand 15 minutes or until soft. Drain well; cut into 3-inch lengths.

3. Meanwhile, heat oil in large skillet over medium-high heat. Add tofu; cook 4 minutes per side or until golden. Remove to paper towel-lined baking sheet.

4. Add jicama to skillet; stir-fry 5 minutes or until lightly browned. Remove to baking sheet. Stir-fry sweet potatoes in batches until tender and browned; remove to baking sheet. Add leeks; stir-fry 1 minute. Remove to baking sheet.

5. Stir soy sauce mixture; add to skillet, stirring until sugar dissolves. Add noodles; toss to coat. Gently stir in tofu, vegetables, peanuts, mint and cilantro; cook until heated through.

Makes 4 servings

Fusilli Pizzaiolo

1 package (16 ounces) uncooked fusilli or rotini pasta
¼ cup olive oil
10 green onions, chopped
8 ounces mushrooms, sliced
1 large red bell pepper, chopped
1 large green bell pepper, chopped
1 large yellow bell pepper, chopped
3 large shallots, chopped
1 large onion, chopped
½ cup chopped fresh basil *or* 2 teaspoons dried basil
8 cloves garlic, minced
2 tablespoons chopped fresh oregano *or* 1 teaspoon dried oregano, crushed
Dash red pepper flakes
4 cups canned tomatoes, undrained, chopped
Salt and black pepper to taste

1. Cook pasta according to package directions; drain and keep warm.

2. Heat oil in large skillet over medium-high heat. Add green onions, mushrooms, bell peppers, shallots, basil, garlic, oregano and red pepper flakes; cook and stir until onions are lightly browned.

3. Add tomatoes with juice; bring to a boil. Reduce heat to low; simmer, uncovered, 20 minutes. Season with salt and black pepper.

4. Add pasta to sauce; toss to coat.

Makes 6 to 8 servings

Spicy Manicotti

3 cups Not-Ricotta (recipe follows)
**⅔ cup vegan Parmesan-flavor topping,
　 plus additional for serving**
1 egg, lightly beaten
2½ tablespoons chopped fresh parsley
1 teaspoon Italian seasoning
½ teaspoon garlic powder
½ teaspoon salt
½ teaspoon black pepper
**12 ounces soy chorizo, meatless Italian sausage
　 or soy crumbles**
1 can (28 ounces) crushed tomatoes
1 jar (26 ounces) marinara sauce
8 ounces uncooked manicotti shells

1. Preheat oven to 375°F. Spray 13×9-inch baking dish with nonstick cooking spray. Prepare Not-Ricotta.

2. For filling, combine Not-Ricotta, ⅔ cup Parmesan-flavor topping, egg, parsley, Italian seasoning, garlic powder, salt and pepper in medium bowl; set aside.

3. Crumble soy chorizo into large skillet; cook and stir over medium-high heat until browned. Remove from skillet; set aside.

4. Add tomatoes and marinara sauce to skillet; bring to a boil over high heat. Reduce heat to low; simmer, uncovered, 10 minutes. Pour about one third of sauce into prepared dish.

5. Stuff each shell with about ½ cup filling. Place in dish. Top shells with sausage; pour remaining sauce over shells.

6. Cover tightly with foil; bake 50 minutes to 1 hour or until pasta is tender. Let stand 5 minutes before serving. Sprinkle with additional Parmesan-flavor topping.

Makes 8 to 10 servings

Not-Ricotta: Crumble 1 package (14 ounces) drained and pressed firm tofu into large bowl. Add 1 cup silken tofu, ½ cup chopped fresh parsley, 2 teaspoons coarse salt, 2 teaspoons lemon juice, 1 teaspoon sugar and 1 teaspoon black peppper; mix well. Refrigerate until needed. Drain liquid before using.

Dairy-Free Mac and Cheez

1½ cups uncooked elbow macaroni
1 cup chopped onion
1 cup chopped red or green bell pepper
¾ cup chopped celery
¾ cup nutritional yeast
¼ cup all-purpose flour
1½ teaspoons salt
¼ teaspoon garlic powder
¼ teaspoon onion powder
2 cups unsweetened soymilk or other dairy-free milk
1 teaspoon yellow mustard
3 drops hot pepper sauce (optional)
½ teaspoon paprika

1. Preheat oven to 350°F. Spray 13×9-inch baking dish with nonstick cooking spray. Prepare macaroni according to package directions; add onion, bell pepper and celery during last 5 minutes of cooking. Drain and return to saucepan.

2. Meanwhile, combine nutritional yeast, flour, salt, garlic powder and onion powder in medium saucepan. Whisk in soymilk over medium heat until smooth. Add mustard and hot pepper sauce, if desired. Continue whisking 10 minutes or until mixture thickens to desired consistency. Pour over macaroni and vegetables; mix well.

3. Spread mixture in prepared baking dish; sprinkle with paprika. Bake 15 to 20 minutes or until heated through.

Makes 4 to 6 servings

Tip: Try this sauce over vegetables for a creamy side dish, or over corn chips for nachos.

Tofu Stuffed Shells

       1 can (15 ounces) tomato purée
       1 package (8 ounces) mushrooms, thinly sliced
       ½ cup shredded carrots
       ¼ cup water
       2 cloves garlic, minced
       1 tablespoon sugar
       1 tablespoon Italian seasoning
      12 uncooked jumbo pasta shells
       1 package (14 ounces) firm tofu, drained and pressed
       ½ cup chopped green onions
       2 tablespoons vegan Parmesan-flavor topping
       2 tablespoons minced fresh parsley
       1 tablespoon dried basil
       ½ teaspoon salt
       ¼ teaspoon black pepper
       ½ cup (2 ounces) shredded dairy-free mozzarella
         cheese alternative

1. For sauce, combine tomato purée, mushrooms, carrots, water, garlic, sugar and Italian seasoning in medium saucepan; bring to a boil over medium heat. Reduce heat to low; cover and simmer 20 minutes, stirring occasionally.

2. Meanwhile, cook shells according to package directions. Rinse under cold water; drain. Spread thin layer of sauce in bottom of 13×9-inch baking pan.

3. Preheat oven to 350°F. Crumble tofu into medium bowl. Stir in green onions, Parmesan-flavor topping, parsley, basil, salt and pepper. Stuff shells with tofu mixture. Place shells, stuffed side up, in single layer in prepared pan. Pour remaining sauce evenly over shells.

4. Cover tightly with foil; bake 30 minutes. Remove foil; sprinkle with dairy-free mozzarella. Bake, uncovered, 5 to 10 minutes or until hot and bubbly.

Makes 4 servings

Mushroom Gratin

4 tablespoons dairy-free margarine, divided
1 small onion, minced
1 package (8 ounces) sliced cremini mushrooms (about 2½ cups)
2 cloves garlic, minced
4 cups cooked elbow macaroni, rotini or other pasta
2 tablespoons all-purpose flour
1 cup unsweetened soymilk
½ teaspoon salt
½ teaspoon black pepper
½ teaspoon dry mustard
½ cup fresh bread crumbs
1 tablespoon extra virgin olive oil

1. Preheat oven to 350°F. Spray shallow baking dish or casserole with nonstick cooking spray. Melt 2 tablespoons margarine in large skillet over medium-high heat. Add onion; cook and stir
2 minutes. Add mushrooms and garlic; cook and stir 6 to 8 minutes or until vegetables soften. Remove from heat; stir in macaroni.

2. Melt remaining 2 tablespoons margarine in medium saucepan over low heat. Whisk in flour; cook and stir 2 minutes without browning. Stir in soymilk. Bring to a boil over medium-high heat, whisking constantly. Reduce heat to a simmer. Add salt, pepper and mustard; whisk 5 to 7 minutes or until sauce thickens.

3. Pour sauce over mushroom mixture in skillet; stir to coat. Spoon into prepared baking dish. Top with bread crumbs; drizzle with oil.

4. Cover and bake 15 minutes. Uncover; bake 10 minutes or until edges are bubbly and top is browned.

Makes 8 servings

Packed with Protein

Tofu, Vegetable and Curry Stir-Fry

1 package (about 14 ounces) extra firm tofu, drained
¾ cup coconut milk
2 tablespoons fresh lime juice
1 tablespoon curry powder
2 teaspoons dark sesame oil, divided
4 cups broccoli florets (1½-inch pieces)
2 medium red bell peppers, cut into short thin strips
1 medium red onion, cut into thin wedges
¼ teaspoon salt
    Hot cooked brown rice (optional)

1. Press tofu cubes between paper towels; cut into ¾-inch cubes. Combine coconut milk, lime juice and curry powder in medium bowl.

2. Heat 1 teaspoon oil in large nonstick skillet over medium heat. Add tofu; cook 10 minutes or until lightly browned on all sides, turning frequently. Remove to plate.

3. Add remaining 1 teaspoon oil to skillet; increase heat to high. Add broccoli, bell pepper and onion; stir-fry about 5 minutes or until vegetables are crisp-tender. Stir in tofu, coconut milk mixture and salt; cook and stir until mixture comes to a boil. Serve immediately with rice, if desired.

Makes 4 servings

Black Bean and Tempeh Burritos

　　2 teaspoons olive oil
　　½ cup chopped onion
　　½ cup chopped green bell pepper
　　2 cloves garlic, minced
　　2 teaspoons chili powder
　　1 can (about 28 ounces) stewed tomatoes
　　1 teaspoon dried oregano
　　½ teaspoon dried coriander
　　1 can (about 15 ounces) black beans, rinsed and drained
　　4 ounces unseasoned tempeh, diced
　　¼ cup minced onion
　　¼ teaspoon black pepper
　　½ teaspoon ground cumin
　　8 (6-inch) flour tortillas

1. For sauce, heat oil in large nonstick skillet over medium heat. Add chopped onion, bell pepper and garlic; cook and stir 5 minutes or until onion is tender. Add chili powder; cook 1 minute. Add tomatoes, oregano and coriander; cook 15 minutes, stirring frequently.

2. Preheat oven to 350°F. Spray 13×9-inch baking dish with nonstick cooking spray. Place beans in medium bowl; mash well with fork. Stir in tempeh, minced onion, black pepper and cumin. Stir in ¼ cup sauce.

3. Soften tortillas if necessary.* Spread ⅓ cup bean mixture down center of each tortilla. Roll up tortillas; place in single layer in shallow baking dish. Top with remaining sauce.

4. Bake 15 minutes or until heated through.

To soften tortillas, wrap stack of tortillas in foil. Heat in preheated 350°F oven about 10 minutes or until softened.

Makes 4 servings

Thai Seitan Stir-Fry

1 package (8 ounces) seitan, drained and thinly sliced
1 jalapeño pepper, halved and seeded
3 cloves garlic
1 piece peeled fresh ginger (about 1 inch)
⅓ cup soy sauce
¼ cup packed brown sugar
¼ cup lime juice
½ teaspoon red pepper flakes
¼ teaspoon salt
3 tablespoons vegetable oil
1 medium onion, chopped
2 red bell peppers, quartered and thinly sliced
2 cups broccoli florets
3 green onions, diagonally sliced
4 cups lightly packed baby spinach
¼ cup shredded fresh basil
3 cups hot cooked rice
¼ cup salted peanuts, chopped

1. Place seitan in medium bowl. Combine jalapeño, garlic and ginger in food processor; process until finely chopped. Add soy sauce, brown sugar, lime juice, red pepper flakes and salt; process until blended. Pour mixture over seitan; toss to coat. Marinate at least 20 minutes at room temperature.

2. Heat oil in wok or large skillet over high heat. Add onion, bell peppers and broccoli; stir-fry 3 to 5 minutes. Add seitan, marinade and green onions; bring to a boil. Cook and stir 3 minutes or until vegetables are crisp-tender and seitan is heated through. Add half of spinach; stir-fry until beginning to wilt. Add remaining spinach; cook just until wilted.

3. Stir in basil just before serving. Serve over rice; sprinkle with peanuts.

Makes 4 to 6 servings

Wild Mushroom Tofu Burgers

2 tablespoons olive oil, divided

1 package (8 ounces) cremini mushrooms, coarsely chopped

½ medium onion, coarsely chopped

1 clove garlic, minced

3 tablespoons water

1 tablespoon flaxseed

7 ounces extra firm tofu, crumbled and frozen*

1 cup old-fashioned oats

⅓ cup finely chopped walnuts

½ teaspoon salt

½ teaspoon onion powder

¼ teaspoon dried thyme

6 multi-grain English muffins, split and toasted

Lettuce, tomato and red onion slices (optional)

*Freeze at least 1 hour.

1. Heat 1 tablespoon oil in large nonstick skillet over medium heat. Add mushrooms, onion and garlic; cook and stir 10 minutes or until mushrooms have released most of their juices. Remove from heat; cool slightly.

2. Meanwhile, combine water and flaxseed in small saucepan; simmer over medium-low heat 5 minutes. Cool to room temperature.

3. Combine mushroom mixture, tofu, oats, walnuts, flaxseed mixture, salt, onion powder and thyme in food processor or blender; process until combined. (Some tofu pieces may remain). Shape mixture into six ⅓-cup patties.

4. Heat half of remaining oil in same skillet over medium-low heat. Working in batches, cook patties 5 minutes per side. Repeat with remaining oil and patties. Serve burgers on English muffins with lettuce, tomato and onion, if desired.

Makes 6 servings

Teriyaki Tempeh with Pineapple

**1 package (8 ounces) unseasoned tempeh,
cut in half crosswise**
1 to 1½ cups pineapple teriyaki sauce
1 cup uncooked rice
½ cup matchstick-size carrots
½ cup snow peas
½ cup matchstick-size red bell pepper strips
4 fresh pineapple rings

1. Place 1 cup water and tempeh in large deep skillet; bring to
a boil over high heat. Reduce heat to low; simmer 10 minutes.
Drain water; add 1 cup teriyaki sauce to tempeh in skillet. Bring
to a simmer over medium heat; simmer 10 minutes, turning
tempeh occasionally. Drain and reserve teriyaki sauce; add
additional sauce, if necessary, to make ½ cup.

2. Meanwhile, cook rice according to package directions.
Heat reserved teriyaki sauce in wok or large nonstick skillet
over medium-high heat. Add carrots, snow peas and bell
pepper; cook and stir 4 to 6 minutes or until crisp-tender. Add
rice; stir to combine. Add additional teriyaki sauce, if desired.

3. Prepare grill for direct cooking. Grill tempeh and pineapple
rings over medium-high heat 10 minutes, turning once. Cut
tempeh in half; serve with rice and pineapple.

Makes 4 servings

Island Tempeh Sandwiches: Omit rice and vegetables. Serve
tempeh and pineapple on soft rolls with arugula, additional
teriyaki sauce and vegan mayonnaise, if desired.

Seitan Fajitas

1 package (1 ounce) fajita seasoning
2 packages (8 ounces each) seitan, sliced
1 tablespoon vegetable oil
1 red bell pepper, sliced
½ medium onion, sliced
1 package (8 ounces) sliced mushrooms
6 (6- to 7-inch) tortillas, warmed
 Salsa, guacamole and shredded dairy-free cheese
 alternative (optional)

1. Dissolve seasoning according to package directions. Place seitan in large resealable food storage bag. Pour seasoning mixture over seitan. Seal bag; shake to coat.

2. Heat oil in large skillet. Add bell pepper and onion; cook and stir 4 to 5 minutes or until crisp-tender. Add mushrooms; cook and stir 4 to 5 minutes or until mushrooms are softened. Add seitan and seasoning mixture; cook and stir 1 to 2 minutes or until seitan is heated through and vegetables are coated with seasoning.

3. Divide vegetable mixture evenly among tortillas. Serve with desired toppings.

Makes 6 fajitas

Tip: You'll find seitan in the refrigerated section of natural food stores and well-stocked supermarkets near the produce section, or in the dairy case in a tub or a vacuum pack. Varieties include plain, seasoned and Asian-style with soy and ginger. If you're going to be seasoning it yourself as part of a recipe, purchase plain seitan.

Soba Stir-Fry

8 ounces uncooked soba (buckwheat) noodles
½ cup vegetable broth
2 tablespoons reduced-sodium tamari or soy sauce
1 tablespoon rice wine or dry sherry
2 teaspoons cornstarch
1 tablespoon olive oil
2 cups sliced shiitake mushrooms
1 medium red bell pepper, cut into thin strips
2 whole dried red chiles *or* ¼ teaspoon red pepper flakes
1 clove garlic, minced
2 cups shredded napa cabbage
1 package (14 ounces) firm tofu, drained and cut into 1-inch cubes
2 green onions, thinly sliced

1. Cook noodles according to package directions; drain and set aside. Whisk broth, tamari and rice wine into cornstarch in small bowl until smooth.

2. Heat oil in large nonstick skillet or wok over medium-high heat. Add mushrooms, bell pepper, dried chiles and garlic; stir-fry 3 minutes or until mushrooms are tender. Add cabbage; cover and cook 2 minutes or until cabbage is wilted. Stir in tofu.

3. Stir sauce; stir into vegetable mixture. Cook 2 minutes or until sauce is thickened.

4. Stir in noodles; toss gently until heated through. Sprinkle with green onions. Serve immediately.

Makes 4 servings

Fried Tofu with Sesame Dipping Sauce

3 tablespoons soy sauce or tamari
2 tablespoons unseasoned rice vinegar
2 teaspoons sugar
1 teaspoon sesame seeds, toasted*
1 teaspoon dark sesame oil
⅛ teaspoon red pepper flakes
1 package (14 ounces) extra firm tofu
2 tablespoons all-purpose flour
¼ cup rice milk or plain soymilk
1 tablespoon cornstarch
¾ cup panko bread crumbs
4 tablespoons vegetable oil

To toast sesame seeds, spread seeds in small skillet. Shake skillet over medium-low heat about 3 minutes or until seeds begin to pop and turn golden.

1. For dipping sauce, combine soy sauce, vinegar, sugar, sesame seeds, sesame oil and red pepper flakes in small bowl. Set aside.

2. Drain tofu and press between paper towels to remove excess water. Cut crosswise into four slices; cut each slice diagonally into triangles. Place flour in shallow dish. Stir rice milk into cornstarch in shallow bowl until smooth. Place panko in another shallow bowl.

3. Dip each piece of tofu in flour to lightly coat all sides; dip in rice milk mixture, turning to coat. Drain; roll in panko to coat.

4. Heat 2 tablespoons vegetable oil in large nonstick skillet over high heat. Reduce heat to medium; add half of tofu in single layer. Cook 1 to 2 minutes per side or until golden brown. Repeat with remaining tofu. Serve with dipping sauce.

Makes 4 servings

Barbecue Seitan Skewers

1 package (8 ounces) unseasoned seitan, cubed
½ cup barbecue sauce, divided
1 red bell pepper, cut into 12 pieces
1 green bell pepper, cut into 12 pieces
12 mushrooms
1 zucchini, cut into 12 pieces

1. Place seitan in medium bowl. Add ¼ cup barbecue sauce; stir to coat. Marinate in refrigerator 30 minutes. Soak four bamboo skewers in water 20 minutes.

2. Oil grid. Prepare grill for direct cooking. Thread seitan, bell peppers, mushrooms and zucchini onto skewers.

3. Grill skewers, covered, over medium-high heat 8 minutes or until seitan is hot and glazed with sauce, brushing with some of remaining sauce and turning occasionally.

Makes 4 servings

Note:

Seitan is a meat substitute made from wheat that has had the starch washed away until only the wheat protein (gluten) remains. It is high in protein and has a meaty, chewy texture. Like tofu and tempeh, it will take on the flavor of whatever you marinate or cook with it.

Tofu Satay with Peanut Sauce

    1 package (14 ounces) firm tofu, drained and pressed*
    ⅓ cup water
    ⅓ cup soy sauce
    1 tablespoon sesame oil
    1 teaspoon minced garlic
    1 teaspoon minced fresh ginger
   24 white button mushrooms, trimmed
    1 large red bell pepper, cut into 12 pieces
    1 can (14 ounces) unsweetened coconut milk
    ½ cup creamy peanut butter
    2 tablespoons packed brown sugar
    1 tablespoon rice vinegar
    1 to 2 teaspoons red Thai curry paste

To press tofu, place between layers of paper towels. Place flat, heavy object on top; let stand 15 to 30 minutes.

1. Cut tofu into 24 cubes. Combine water, soy sauce, sesame oil, garlic and ginger in small bowl. Place tofu, mushrooms and bell pepper in large resealable food storage bag. Add soy sauce mixture; seal bag and turn gently to coat. Marinate 30 minutes, turning occasionally. Soak eight 8-inch bamboo skewers in water 20 minutes.

2. Preheat oven to 400°F. Spray 13×9-inch glass baking dish with nonstick cooking spray.

3. Drain tofu mixture; discard marinade. Thread skewers, alternating tofu with mushrooms and bell pepper. Place skewers in prepared baking dish.

4. Bake 25 minutes or until tofu cubes are lightly browned and vegetables are softened.

5. Meanwhile, for peanut sauce, whisk coconut milk, peanut butter, brown sugar, vinegar and curry paste in small saucepan over medium heat. Bring to a boil, stirring constantly. Immediately reduce heat to low; cook about 20 minutes or until thick and creamy, stirring frequently. Serve satay with sauce.

Makes 4 servings

Beans & Grains

Meatless Sloppy Joes

1 tablespoon olive oil

2 cups thinly sliced onions

2 cups chopped green bell peppers

2 cloves garlic, finely chopped

2 tablespoons ketchup

1 tablespoon yellow mustard

1 can (about 15 ounces) kidney beans, rinsed, drained and mashed

1 can (8 ounces) tomato sauce

1 teaspoon chili powder

Cider vinegar

4 sandwich rolls, split

1. Heat oil in large nonstick skillet over medium heat. Add onions, bell peppers and garlic; cook and stir 5 minutes or until vegetables are tender. Stir in ketchup and mustard.

2. Reduce heat to medium-low. Add beans, tomato sauce and chili powder; cook about 5 minutes or until thickened, stirring frequently and adding up to ⅓ cup vinegar if dry. Serve bean mixture in rolls.

Makes 4 servings

Bulgur with Asparagus and Spring Herbs

⅔ cup uncooked bulgur
2 cups sliced asparagus (1-inch pieces)
½ cup frozen peas, thawed
⅔ cup chopped fresh Italian parsley
2 teaspoons finely chopped fresh mint
3 tablespoons lemon juice
1 tablespoon orange juice
1 tablespoon extra virgin olive oil
¼ teaspoon salt
⅛ teaspoon black pepper

1. Prepare bulgur according to package directions; drain well.

2. Steam asparagus in steamer basket over boiling water 3 to 4 minutes or until bright green and crisp-tender. Cool under cold running water; drain well and blot with paper towels.

3. Combine bulgur, asparagus, peas, parsley and mint in large bowl. Whisk lemon juice, orange juice, oil, salt and pepper in small bowl. Pour over bulgur mixture; toss gently.

Makes 4 servings

Note: Bulgur is a whole grain that's high in fiber and protein. It's also a good source of iron, magnesium, and B vitamins.

Jambalaya-Style Rice

2 cups chopped green bell peppers

1 can (about 15 ounces) dark red kidney beans, rinsed and drained

1 can (about 14 ounces) diced tomatoes with green bell peppers and onions

1 cup chopped onion

1 cup sliced celery

1 cup water, divided

¾ cup uncooked long grain white rice

1¼ teaspoons salt

1 teaspoon hot pepper sauce

½ teaspoon dried thyme

½ teaspoon red pepper flakes

3 bay leaves

8 ounces meatless burgers, thawed if frozen

2 tablespoons extra virgin olive oil

½ cup chopped fresh parsley

Slow Cooker Directions

1. Combine bell peppers, beans, tomatoes, onion, celery, ½ cup water, rice, salt, hot pepper sauce, thyme, red pepper flakes and bay leaves in slow cooker. Cover; cook on LOW 4 to 5 hours. Remove and discard bay leaves.

2. Dice burgers. Heat oil in large nonstick skillet over medium-high heat. Add burgers; cook 2 minutes or until lightly browned, scraping bottom of skillet occasionally.

3. Transfer to slow cooker. *Do not stir.* Add remaining ½ cup water to skillet; bring to a boil over high heat 1 minute, scraping up bits from bottom of skillet. Add liquid and parsley to slow cooker; stir gently to blend. Serve immediately.

Makes 4 to 6 servings

Four-Pepper Black Bean Fajitas

1 can (about 15 ounces) black beans,
   rinsed and drained
¼ cup water
3 tablespoons olive oil, divided
2 tablespoons lime juice
1 canned chipotle pepper in adobo sauce
1 clove garlic, minced
½ teaspoon salt
1 medium red bell pepper, cut into strips
1 medium green bell pepper, cut into strips
1 medium yellow bell pepper, cut into strips
2 medium onions, cut into ¼-inch wedges
8 (8-inch) flour tortillas
¼ cup chopped fresh cilantro
   Lime wedges (optional)

1. Combine beans, water, 2 tablespoons oil, lime juice, chipotle, garlic and salt in food processor or blender; process until smooth. Place in medium microwavable bowl. Cover with plastic wrap; set aside.

2. Heat remaining 1 tablespoon oil in large skillet over medium-high heat. Add bell peppers and onions; cook and stir 12 minutes or until vegetables begin to brown.

3. Microwave bean mixture on HIGH 2 to 3 minutes or until heated through. Heat tortillas according to package directions.

4. Divide bean mixture among tortillas; top with bell pepper mixture. Sprinkle with cilantro; serve with lime wedges, if desired.

Makes 4 servings

Millet Pilaf

1 tablespoon olive oil
½ onion, finely chopped
½ red bell pepper, finely chopped
1 carrot, finely chopped
2 cloves garlic, minced
1 cup uncooked millet
3 cups water
    Grated peel and juice of 1 lemon
¾ teaspoon salt
½ teaspoon black pepper
2 tablespoons chopped fresh parsley (optional)

1. Heat oil in medium saucepan over medium heat. Add onion, bell pepper, carrot and garlic; cook and stir 5 minutes or until softened. Add millet; cook and stir 5 minutes or until lightly toasted.

2. Stir in water, lemon peel, lemon juice, salt and black pepper; bring to a boil. Reduce heat to low; cover and simmer 30 minutes or until water is absorbed and millet is tender. Cover and let stand 5 minutes. Fluff with fork. Sprinkle with parsley, if desired.

Makes 6 servings

Black Bean Sliders

6 tablespoons water
2 tablespoons ground flaxseed
1 can (about 15 ounces) black beans,
     rinsed and drained
2 cloves garlic
½ teaspoon salt
½ cup chopped onion
½ cup chopped red bell pepper
2 tablespoons chopped fresh parsley
1 cup plain dry bread crumbs
32 mini whole wheat pita bread rounds, split
Sliced avocado and/or salsa (optional)

1. Combine water and flaxseed in small saucepan; simmer over medium-low heat 5 minutes. Cool to room temperature.

2. Preheat oven to 375°F. Spray baking sheet with nonstick cooking spray.

3. Combine beans, flaxseed mixture, garlic and salt in food processor or blender; process just until smooth. Add onion, bell pepper and parsley; pulse until combined. Stir in bread crumbs.

4. Shape mixture into 32 (1-inch) patties. Place on prepared baking sheet. Spray patties with cooking spray.

5. Bake 10 minutes. Turn and bake 10 minutes or tops are firm and browned. Serve in pita with avocado and salsa, if desired.

Makes 32 sliders

Paella

2 teaspoons canola oil
1 cup chopped onion
2 cloves garlic, minced
1 cup brown rice
2¼ cups vegetable broth
1 teaspoon Italian seasoning
¾ teaspoon salt
½ teaspoon ground turmeric
⅛ teaspoon ground red pepper
1 can (about 14 ounces) stewed tomatoes
1 cup chopped red bell pepper
1 cup coarsely chopped carrots
1 can (14 ounces) quartered artichoke hearts, drained
1 small zucchini, halved lengthwise and cut into ¼-inch slices (about 1¼ cups)
½ cup frozen peas

1. Heat oil in large nonstick skillet over medium-high heat. Add onion and garlic; cook and stir 6 to 7 minutes or until onion is translucent. Reduce heat to over medium-low. Add rice; cook and stir 1 minute.

2. Add broth, Italian seasoning, salt, turmeric and ground red pepper; bring to a boil over medium-high heat. Reduce heat to low; cover and simmer 30 minutes.

3. Stir in tomatoes, bell pepper and carrots; cover and simmer 10 minutes.

4. Add artichokes, zucchini and peas; cover and cook 10 minutes or until vegetables are crisp-tender.

Makes 6 servings

Quinoa Burrito Bowls

1 cup uncooked quinoa
2 cups water
2 tablespoons fresh lime juice, divided
½ teaspoon salt
¼ cup vegan sour cream
2 teaspoons vegetable oil
1 small onion, diced
1 red bell pepper, diced
1 clove garlic, minced
½ cup canned black beans, rinsed and drained
½ cup thawed frozen corn
    Shredded lettuce
    Lime wedges (optional)

1. Place quinoa in fine-mesh strainer; rinse well under cold running water. Bring 2 cups water to a boil in small saucepan over high heat; stir in quinoa. Reduce heat to low; cover and simmer 10 to 15 minutes or until quinoa is tender and water is absorbed. Stir in 1 tablespoon lime juice and salt. Cover and keep warm.

2. Combine sour cream and remaining 1 tablespoon lime juice in small bowl; set aside.

3. Heat oil in large skillet over medium heat. Add onion and bell pepper; cook and stir 5 minutes or until softened. Add garlic; cook and stir 1 minute. Add beans and corn; cook and stir 3 to 5 minutes or until heated through.

4. Divide quinoa among four bowls; top with bean mixture, lettuce and sour cream mixture. Garnish with lime wedges.

Makes 4 servings

Farro Veggie Burgers

1½ cups water
½ cup pearled farro or spelt
2 medium potatoes, peeled and quartered
2 to 4 tablespoons canola oil, divided
¾ cup finely chopped green onions
1 cup grated carrots
2 teaspoons grated fresh ginger
2 tablespoons ground almonds
¾ teaspoon salt
¼ teaspoon black pepper
½ cup panko bread crumbs
6 whole wheat hamburger buns
Ketchup and mustard (optional)

1. Combine 1½ cups water and farro in medium saucepan; bring to a boil over high heat. Reduce heat to low; partially cover and cook 25 to 30 minutes or until farro is tender. Drain and cool. (If using spelt, use 2 cups water and cook until tender.)

2. Meanwhile, place potatoes in large saucepan; cover with water. Bring to a boil; reduce heat and simmer 20 minutes or until tender. Cool and mash potatoes; set aside.

3. Heat 1 tablespoon oil in medium skillet over medium-high heat. Add green onions; cook and stir 1 minute. Add carrots and ginger; cover and cook 2 to 3 minutes or until carrots are tender. Transfer to large bowl; cool completely.

4. Add mashed potatoes and farro to carrot mixture. Add almonds, salt and pepper; mix well. Shape mixture into six patties. Spread panko on medium plate; coat patties with panko.

5. Heat 1 tablespoon oil in large nonstick skillet over medium heat. Cook patties about 4 minutes per side or until golden brown, adding additional oil as needed. Serve on buns with desired condiments.

Makes 6 servings

Lentil Rice Curry

2 tablespoons olive oil
1 cup sliced green onions
3 cloves garlic, minced
2 tablespoons minced fresh ginger
2 teaspoons curry powder
½ teaspoon ground cumin
½ teaspoon ground turmeric
3 cups water
1 can (about 14 ounces) stewed tomatoes, undrained
½ teaspoon salt
1 cup dried red lentils, rinsed and sorted
1 large head cauliflower, broken into florets
1 tablespoon lemon juice
Fragrant Basmati Rice (recipe follows) *or* 4 cups hot cooked jasmine rice

1. Heat oil in large saucepan over medium heat. Add green onions, garlic, ginger, curry powder, cumin and turmeric; cook and stir 5 minutes. Add water, tomatoes and salt; bring to a boil over high heat.

2. Stir in lentils. Reduce heat to low; cover and simmer 35 to 40 minutes or until lentils are tender. Add cauliflower and lemon juice; cover and simmer 8 to 10 minutes or until cauliflower is tender.

3. Meanwhile prepare Fragrant Basmati Rice, if desired. Serve with lentil curry.

Makes 6 servings

Fragrant Basmati Rice: Bring 2 cups apple juice, ¾ cup water and ½ teaspoon salt to a boil in medium saucepan over high heat. Add 1½ cups white basmati rice, 2 thin slices fresh ginger and 1 (2-inch) cinnamon stick; cover and simmer over low heat 25 to 30 minutes or until liquid is absorbed. Remove and discard ginger and cinnamon stick. Makes 4 cups.

Vegetable Bliss

Apple Stuffed Acorn Squash

¼ **cup raisins**
2 **medium acorn squash**
2½ **tablespoons dairy-free margarine, melted, divided**
2 **tablespoons sugar**
¼ **teaspoon ground cinnamon**
2 **medium Fuji apples, cut into ¼-inch pieces**

1. Place raisins in small bowl; cover with warm water and soak 20 minutes. Preheat oven to 375°F.

2. Cut squash into quarters; remove seeds. Place squash on baking sheet; brush with ½ tablespoon margarine. Combine sugar and cinnamon in small bowl; sprinkle half of cinnamon mixture over squash. Bake 10 minutes.

3. Meanwhile, drain raisins. Heat remaining 2 tablespoons margarine in medium skillet over medium heat. Add apples, raisins and remaining cinnamon mixture; cook and stir 2 minutes. Top partially baked squash with apple mixture.

4. Bake 30 to 35 minutes or until apples and squash are tender. Serve warm.

Makes 4 servings

Spring Vegetable Ragoût

1 tablespoon olive oil
2 leeks, thinly sliced
3 cloves garlic, minced
1 package (10 ounces) frozen corn
8 ounces yellow squash, halved lengthwise and cut into ½-inch pieces (about 1¼ cups)
1 cup vegetable broth
6 ounces frozen shelled edamame
1 small package (4 ounces) shredded carrots
3 cups small cherry tomatoes, halved
1 teaspoon dried tarragon
1 teaspoon dried basil
1 teaspoon dried oregano
Salt and black pepper
Minced fresh parsley (optional)

1. Heat oil in large skillet over medium heat. Add leeks and garlic; cook and stir 2 minutes. Add corn, squash, broth, edamame and carrots; cook and stir about 5 minutes or until squash is tender.

2. Stir in tomatoes, tarragon, basil and oregano. Reduce heat to low; cover and simmer 2 minutes or until tomatoes are soft. Season with salt and pepper. Garnish with parsley.

Makes 6 servings

Far East Tabbouleh

1¾ cups boiling water
¾ cup uncooked bulgur wheat
2 tablespoons lemon juice
2 tablespoons reduced-sodium teriyaki sauce
1 tablespoon olive oil
¾ cup diced seeded cucumber
¾ cup diced seeded tomato
½ cup thinly sliced green onions
½ cup minced fresh cilantro or parsley
1 tablespoon minced fresh ginger
1 clove garlic, minced

1. Combine water and bulgur in small bowl. Cover with plastic wrap; let stand 45 minutes or until bulgur is puffed, stirring occasionally. Drain in fine mesh sieve.

2. Combine bulgur, lemon juice, teriyaki sauce and oil in large bowl; mix well. Stir in cucumber, tomato, green onions, cilantro, ginger and garlic until well blended. Cover and refrigerate 4 hours, stirring occasionally.

Makes 4 servings

Vegetarian Shepherd's Pie

2 teaspoons olive oil
1 cup sliced onion
1 package (16 ounces) mushrooms, quartered
1 cup sliced carrots
1 cup sliced celery
1 cup frozen peas
1¼ teaspoons minced garlic, divided
¼ cup all-purpose flour
3 cups vegetable broth
½ teaspoon salt
¼ teaspoon dried rosemary
2 medium russet potatoes, peeled and cubed
¼ cup dairy-free milk
1 tablespoon dairy-free margarine
¼ teaspoon black pepper

1. Heat oil in large saucepan over medium-high heat. Add onion; cook and stir 3 minutes. Add mushrooms; cook and stir 5 minutes or until vegetables are tender. Add carrots, celery and peas and 1 teaspoon garlic; cook and stir 5 minutes or until crisp-tender.

2. Sprinkle flour over vegetables; cook and stir 2 minutes. Add broth, salt and rosemary; bring to a boil. Reduce heat to low; simmer 30 to 35 minutes or until thickened.

3. Meanwhile, place potatoes in medium saucepan; add cold water to cover. Bring to a boil over high heat. Reduce heat to low; simmer 15 minutes or until potatoes are tender. Drain.

4. Beat potatoes, dairy-free milk, margarine, remaining ¼ teaspoon garlic and pepper in medium bowl with electric mixer at low speed until smooth. Preheat broiler.

5. Pour vegetable mixture into 2-quart casserole; gently spread mashed potatoes over top. Broil 5 minutes or until light golden brown.

Makes 6 servings

Mediterranean Pita Pizzas

1 cup chopped peeled cucumber
1 to 2 tablespoons lemon juice
1 tablespoon chopped fresh oregano
½ cup roasted red pepper hummus
4 (6-inch) dairy-free pita bread rounds, warmed
½ cup chopped tomato
¼ cup sliced olives
¼ cup crumbled dairy-free feta cheese
  or Dairy-Free Feta (recipe follows)

1. Combine cucumber, lemon juice and oregano in small bowl.

2. Spread hummus evenly over pita. Top with cucumber mixture, tomato, olives and dairy-free feta.

Makes 4 servings

Dairy-Free Feta: Cut 1 (14-ounce) package firm or extra firm tofu crosswise into two pieces, each about 1 inch thick. Place on paper towel-lined cutting board; top with layer of paper towels. Place weighted baking dish on top of tofu. Let stand 20 minutes. Pat tofu dry and crumble into large bowl. Combine ¼ cup extra virgin olive oil, 2 tablespoons lemon juice, 2 teaspoons Greek seasoning, 1½ teaspoons salt, 1 teaspoon onion powder, ½ teaspoon garlic powder and ½ teaspoon black pepper in small jar with lid; shake to combine well. Pour over tofu and toss gently. Refrigerate 2 hours or overnight. Makes about 2 cups.

Roasted Vegetable Salad with Capers and Walnuts

1 pound small brussels sprouts, trimmed

1 pound unpeeled small Yukon Gold potatoes, halved

½ teaspoon salt

¼ teaspoon black pepper

¼ teaspoon dried rosemary

5 tablespoons olive oil, divided

1 red bell pepper, cut into bite-size pieces

¼ cup walnuts, coarsely chopped

2 tablespoons capers, drained

1½ tablespoons white wine vinegar

1. Preheat oven to 400°F.

2. Slash bottoms of brussels sprouts; place in shallow roasting pan. Add potatoes; sprinkle with salt, black pepper and rosemary. Drizzle with 3 tablespoons oil; toss to coat.

3. Roast 20 minutes. Stir in bell pepper; roast 15 minutes or until tender. Transfer to large bowl; stir in walnuts and capers.

3. Whisk remaining 2 tablespoons oil and vinegar in small bowl until blended. Pour over salad; toss to coat. Serve at room temperature.

Makes 6 to 8 servings

Szechuan Eggplant

1 pound Asian eggplants or regular eggplant, peeled
2 tablespoons peanut or vegetable oil
2 cloves garlic, minced
¼ teaspoon red pepper flakes
¼ cup vegetable broth
¼ cup hoisin sauce
3 green onions, cut into 1-inch pieces
Toasted sesame seeds*

To toast sesame seeds, spread seeds in small skillet. Shake skillet over medium-low heat 3 minutes or until seeds begin to pop and turn golden.

1. Cut eggplants lengthwise into ½-inch slices; cut each slice into ½-inch strips.

2. Heat wok or large nonstick skillet over medium-high heat. Add oil; heat until hot. Add eggplant, garlic and red pepper flakes; stir-fry 7 minutes or until eggplant is very tender and browned.

3. Reduce heat to medium. Add broth, hoisin sauce and green onions; cook and stir 2 minutes. Sprinkle with sesame seeds.

Makes 4 to 6 servings

Parsnip Patties

1 pound parsnips, peeled and cut into ¾-inch chunks
4 tablespoons dairy-free margarine, divided
¼ cup chopped onion
¼ cup all-purpose flour
⅓ cup dairy-free milk
2 teaspoons chopped fresh chives, plus additional for garnish
Salt and black pepper
¾ cup fresh bread crumbs
2 tablespoons vegetable oil

1. Fill medium saucepan with 1 inch of water; bring to a boil over high heat. Add parsnips; cover and cook 10 minutes or until fork-tender. Drain. Place in large bowl; coarsely mash with fork.

2. Melt 2 tablespoons margarine in same saucepan over medium-high heat. Add onion; cook and stir until translucent. Whisk in flour until bubbly and lightly browned. Whisk in dairy-free milk; cook and stir until thickened. Stir into mashed parsnips. Stir in chives; season with salt and pepper.

3. Shape parsnip mixture into four patties. Spread bread crumbs on plate; coat patties with bread crumbs. Place on waxed paper-lined plate; refrigerate 2 hours.

4. Heat remaining 2 tablespoons margarine and oil in large skillet over medium-high heat until margarine is melted and bubbly. Add patties; cook 5 minutes per side or until browned. Sprinkle with additional chives, if desired.

Makes 4 servings

Greek Salad with Dairy-Free "Feta"

Dairy-Free "Feta"

> **1 package (14 ounces) firm or extra firm tofu**
> **½ cup extra virgin olive oil**
> **¼ cup lemon juice**
> **2 teaspoons salt**
> **2 teaspoons Greek or Italian seasoning**
> **½ teaspoon black pepper**
> **1 teaspoon onion powder**
> **½ teaspoon garlic powder**

Salad

> **1 pint grape tomatoes, halved**
> **2 seedless cucumbers, quartered lengthwise and sliced**
> **1 yellow bell pepper, slivered**
> **1 small red onion, cut in thin slices**

1. For "feta," cut tofu crosswise into two pieces, each about 1 inch thick. Place on paper towel-lined cutting board; top with layer of paper towels. Place weighted baking dish on top of tofu; let stand 30 minutes to drain. Pat tofu dry and crumble into large bowl.

2. Combine oil, lemon juice, salt, Greek seasoning and black pepper in small jar with lid; shake until well blended. Reserve ¼ cup mixture for salad dressing. Add onion powder and garlic powder to remaining mixture; pour over tofu and toss gently. Cover and refrigerate 2 hours or overnight.

3. For salad, combine tomatoes, cucumbers, bell pepper and onion in serving bowl. Add tofu and reserved dressing; toss gently.

Makes 4 to 6 servings

Middle Eastern Grilled Vegetable Wraps

1 medium red bell pepper, quartered
1 medium green bell pepper, quartered
1 large eggplant (about 1 pound), cut crosswise into ¼-inch slices
2 tablespoons olive oil
12 ounces large fresh mushrooms
2 green onions, sliced
¼ cup fresh lemon juice
½ teaspoon salt
⅛ teaspoon black pepper
4 (10-inch) flour tortillas
½ cup (4 ounces) hummus
⅓ cup lightly packed fresh cilantro
12 large fresh basil leaves
12 large fresh mint leaves

1. Prepare grill for direct cooking.

2. Grill bell peppers, skin side down, over high heat until skins are blackened. Place in paper bag; close bag. Let stand 5 to 10 minutes or until cool enough to handle. Peel peppers.

3. Lightly brush eggplant with half of oil. Thread mushrooms onto metal skewers; brush with remaining oil. Grill eggplant and mushrooms, covered, over medium heat about 4 minutes or until tender and lightly browned, turning once.

4. Cut eggplant and bell peppers into ½-inch strips; cut mushrooms into quarters. Combine vegetables, green onions, lemon juice, salt and black pepper in medium bowl.

5. Grill tortillas about 1 minute or until warm, turning once. Spoon 2 tablespoons hummus down center of each tortilla. Top with one fourth of cilantro, 3 basil leaves, 3 mint leaves and one fourth of vegetables. Roll to enclose filling; serve immediately.

Makes 4 servings

Table of Contents

Teatime Treats

Banana Bran Bread

1 cup bran cereal
½ cup boiling water
1⅓ cups all-purpose flour
½ cup sugar
1 teaspoon baking powder
½ teaspoon baking soda
½ teaspoon salt
¼ teaspoon ground cinnamon
2 tablespoons vegetable oil
    Prepared egg replacer equal to 2 eggs
1 cup mashed ripe bananas (2 medium bananas)
¼ cup crumbled unsweetened banana chips

1. Preheat oven to 350°F. Spray 8×4-inch loaf pan with nonstick cooking spray. Place cereal into medium bowl; stir in boiling water. Let stand 10 minutes.

2. Combine flour, sugar, baking powder, baking soda, salt and cinnamon in large bowl. Whisk oil and egg replacer in small bowl; add to flour mixture. Stir in bran mixture and mashed bananas. Pour batter into prepared pan. Sprinkle with banana chips.

3. Bake 45 to 50 minutes or until toothpick inserted into center comes out clean. Cool in pan 5 minutes; remove to wire rack to cool completely.

Makes 1 loaf

Orange Cinnamon Rolls

½ cup packed brown sugar
3 tablespoons dairy-free margarine, melted, divided
1 tablespoon ground cinnamon
1 teaspoon grated orange peel
1 loaf (1 pound) frozen bread dough, thawed
⅓ cup raisins (optional)
½ cup powdered sugar, sifted
1 to 2 tablespoons fresh orange juice

1. Spray two 8-inch round cake pans with nonstick cooking spray. Combine brown sugar, 1 tablespoon margarine, cinnamon and orange peel in small bowl; mix well.

2. Roll out dough into 18×8-inch rectangle on lightly floured surface. Brush dough with remaining 2 tablespoons margarine; spread with brown sugar mixture. Sprinkle with raisins, if desired. Starting with long side, roll up dough jelly-roll style; pinch seam to seal. Cut crosswise into 1-inch slices; arrange slices cut sides down in prepared pans. Cover loosely with plastic wrap. Let rise in warm place 30 to 40 minutes or until almost doubled in size. Preheat oven to 350°F.

3. Bake 18 minutes or until golden brown. Immediately remove to wire racks; cool slightly.

4. Whisk powdered sugar and 1 tablespoon orange juice in small bowl until smooth. Add additional orange juice if needed until glaze reaches desired consistency. Drizzle glaze over warm rolls.

Makes 18 rolls

Blueberry Poppy Seed Coffeecake

¾ cup plain soymilk or other dairy-free milk
1 tablespoon lemon juice or vinegar
1½ cups all-purpose flour
½ cup sugar
1 teaspoon baking powder
½ teaspoon baking soda
¼ teaspoon salt
¼ cup (½ stick) cold dairy-free margarine, cut into small pieces
1 tablespoon poppy seeds
Prepared egg replacer equal to 1 egg
1 teaspoon vanilla
1 teaspoon grated lemon peel
1 cup fresh blueberries

1. Preheat oven to 350°F. Spray 9-inch round cake pan with nonstick cooking spray. Combine soymilk and lemon juice in measuring cup. Let stand 5 minutes.

2. Combine flour, sugar, baking powder, baking soda and salt in large bowl. Cut in margarine using pastry blender or two knives until mixture resembles coarse crumbs. Stir in poppy seeds.

3. Whisk soymilk mixture, egg replacer, vanilla and lemon peel in small bowl until blended. Stir into flour mixture just until combined. Spread half of batter in prepared pan; top with blueberries. Drop remaining batter in dollops over blueberries, leaving some berries uncovered.

4. Bake 33 to 36 minutes or until top is golden brown. Cool in pan on wire rack 15 minutes. Serve warm.

Makes 8 servings

Pumpkin Chocolate Chip Muffins

6 tablespoons water
2 tablespoons ground flaxseed
2½ cups all-purpose flour
1 tablespoon baking powder
1½ teaspoons pumpkin pie spice*
½ teaspoon salt
1 cup solid-pack pumpkin
1 cup packed brown sugar
¾ cup vanilla or plain soymilk
6 tablespoons dairy-free margarine, melted
1 cup semisweet chocolate chips
½ cup chopped walnuts

Or substitute ¾ teaspoon ground cinnamon, ½ teaspoon ground ginger and ¼ teaspoon each ground allspice and ground nutmeg.

1. Preheat oven to 400°F. Line 18 standard (2½-inch) muffin cups with paper baking cups or spray with nonstick cooking spray.

2. Combine water and flaxseed in small saucepan; simmer over medium-low heat 5 minutes. Cool to room temperature.

3. Combine flour, baking powder, pumpkin pie spice and salt in large bowl. Beat pumpkin, brown sugar, soymilk, margarine and flaxseed mixture in medium bowl until well blended. Add pumpkin mixture, chocolate chips and walnuts to flour mixture; stir just until moistened. Spoon batter evenly into prepared muffin cups.

4. Bake 18 to 22 minutes or until toothpick inserted into centers comes out clean. Cool in pans on wire racks 10 minutes; remove to wire racks to cool completely.

Makes 18 muffins

Boston Black Coffee Bread

½ **cup rye flour**
½ **cup cornmeal**
½ **cup whole wheat flour**
1 **teaspoon baking soda**
½ **teaspoon salt**
¾ **cup strong brewed coffee, room temperature or cold**
⅓ **cup molasses**
¼ **cup canola oil**
¾ **cup raisins**

1. Preheat oven to 325°F. Grease and flour 9×5-inch loaf pan.

2. Combine rye flour, cornmeal, whole wheat flour, baking soda and salt in large bowl. Add coffee, molasses and oil; stir until blended. Fold in raisins. Pour batter into prepared pan.

3. Bake 50 minutes or until toothpick inserted into center comes out clean. Cool completely in pan on wire rack.

Makes 1 loaf

Tip:

To cool hot coffee, pour it over 2 ice cubes in a measuring cup to measure ¾ cup total. Let stand 10 minutes to cool.

Peach Streusel Coffeecake

3 tablespoons water
1 tablespoon ground flaxseed
2½ cups biscuit baking mix, divided
⅔ cup vanilla or plain soymilk
¼ cup granulated sugar
1 teaspoon ground cinnamon
1 teaspoon vanilla
1 pound frozen unsweetened peaches, thawed
  and diced
½ cup packed dark brown sugar
3 tablespoons cold dairy-free margarine, diced
½ cup pecan pieces

1. Preheat oven to 375°F. Spray 9-inch square baking pan with nonstick cooking spray.

2. Combine water and flaxseed in small saucepan; simmer over medium-low heat 5 minutes. Cool to room temperature.

3. For coffeecake, place 2 cups baking mix in medium bowl; break up lumps with spoon. Add soymilk, flaxseed mixture, granulated sugar, cinnamon and vanilla; stir until well blended. Add peaches; stir just until blended. Pour batter into prepared pan.

4. For topping, combine remaining ½ cup baking mix and brown sugar in small bowl; stir until well blended. Cut in margarine with pastry blender or two knives until coarse crumbs form. Stir in pecans. Sprinkle evenly over batter.

5. Bake 35 minutes or until toothpick inserted into center comes out clean. Cool in pan on wire rack 15 minutes. Serve warm or at room temperature.

Makes 9 servings

Ginger Squash Muffins

    3 tablespoons water
    1 tablespoon ground flaxseed
1½ cups all-purpose flour
    ⅓ cup whole wheat flour
    ⅓ cup granulated sugar
    ¼ cup packed dark brown sugar
2½ teaspoons baking powder
    2 teaspoons ground ginger
    1 teaspoon ground cinnamon
    ¾ teaspoon salt
    ½ teaspoon baking soda
    1 cup frozen winter squash, thawed*
    ⅓ cup canola oil
    ¼ cup finely chopped walnuts
    2 tablespoons finely chopped crystallized ginger
        (optional)

One 12-ounce package of frozen squash yields about 1 cup squash. Or, use puréed cooked fresh butternut squash.

1. Preheat oven to 375°F. Spray 12 standard (2½-inch) muffin cups with nonstick cooking spray. Combine water and flaxseed in small saucepan; simmer over medium-low heat 5 minutes. Cool to room temperature.

2. Combine all-purpose flour, whole wheat flour, granulated sugar, brown sugar, baking powder, ginger, cinnamon, salt and baking soda in large bowl; mix well.

3. Combine squash, flaxseed mixture and oil in small bowl until well blended. Add to flour mixture; stir just until blended. *Do not beat.* Stir in walnuts and crystallized ginger, if desired. Spoon batter evenly into prepared muffin cups.

4. Bake 20 to 25 minutes or until toothpick inserted into centers comes out clean. Cool in pan on wire rack 5 minutes; remove to wire rack to cool completely.

Makes 12 muffins

Chocolate Chip Elvis Bread

3 tablespoons water
1 tablespoon ground flaxseed
2½ cups all-purpose flour
½ cup granulated sugar
½ cup packed brown sugar
1 tablespoon baking powder
¾ teaspoon salt
1 cup mashed ripe bananas (about 2 large)
1 cup vanilla soymilk
¾ cup peanut butter
¼ cup vegetable oil
1 teaspoon vanilla
1 cup semisweet chocolate chips

1. Preheat oven to 350°F. Spray two 8×4-inch loaf pans with nonstick cooking spray.

2. Combine water and flaxseed in small saucepan; simmer over medium-low heat 5 minutes. Cool to room temperature.

3. Combine flour, granulated sugar, brown sugar, baking powder and salt in large bowl; mix well. Beat bananas, soymilk, peanut butter, oil, vanilla and flaxseed mixture in medium bowl until well blended. Add banana mixture and chocolate chips to flour mixture; stir just until moistened. Pour into prepared pans.

4. Bake 40 minutes or until toothpick inserted into centers comes out clean. Cool in pans on wire racks 10 minutes; remove to wire racks to cool completely.

Makes 2 loaves

Cookies & Bars

All-American Chocolate Chip Cookies

2 cups all-purpose flour
1 teaspoon baking soda
½ teaspoon salt
1 cup (2 sticks) dairy-free margarine, softened
¾ cup packed brown sugar
½ cup granulated sugar
½ cup silken tofu, stirred until smooth
1 tablespoon vanilla
2 cups semisweet chocolate chips
1 cup chopped walnuts

1. Preheat oven to 325°F. Line cookie sheets with parchment paper. Combine flour, baking soda and salt in medium bowl.

2. Beat margarine, brown sugar and granulated sugar in large bowl with electric mixer at medium speed about 5 minutes or until light and fluffy. Add tofu; beat until well blended. Beat in vanilla. Add flour mixture; beat until blended. Stir in chocolate chips and walnuts. Drop dough by heaping teaspoonfuls 2 inches apart onto prepared cookie sheets.

3. Bake 8 to 10 minutes or until golden brown. Cool on cookie sheets 2 minutes; remove to wire racks to cool completely.

Makes about 4 dozen cookies

Cranberry Coconut Bars

2 cups fresh or frozen cranberries
1 cup dried cranberries
⅔ cup granulated sugar
¼ cup water
Grated peel of 1 lemon
1¼ cups all-purpose flour
¾ cup old-fashioned oats
½ teaspoon baking soda
½ teaspoon salt
1 cup packed brown sugar
¾ cup (1½ sticks) dairy-free margarine, softened
1 cup flaked coconut
1 cup chopped pecans, toasted*

To toast pecans, spread in single layer on baking sheet. Bake in preheated 350°F oven 5 to 7 minutes or until golden brown, stirring frequently.

1. Preheat oven to 400°F. Grease and flour 13×9-inch baking pan.

2. Combine fresh cranberries, dried cranberries, granulated sugar, water and lemon peel in medium saucepan. Cook over medium-high heat 10 to 15 minutes or until cranberries begin to pop, stirring frequently. Mash cranberries with back of spoon. Let stand 10 minutes.

3. Combine flour, oats, baking soda and salt in medium bowl. Beat brown sugar and margarine in large bowl with electric mixer at medium speed until creamy. Add flour mixture; beat at low speed just until blended. Stir in coconut and pecans. Reserve 1½ cups for topping; press remaining crumb mixture into bottom of prepared pan. Bake 10 minutes.

4. Gently spread cranberry filling evenly over crust. Sprinkle with reserved crumb mixture. Bake 18 to 20 minutes or until center is set and top is golden brown. Cool completely in pan on wire rack. Cut into bars.

Makes 2 dozen bars

Pumpkin Oatmeal Cookies

1 cup all-purpose flour
1 teaspoon ground cinnamon
½ teaspoon salt
½ teaspoon ground nutmeg
¼ teaspoon baking soda
1½ cups packed brown sugar
½ cup (1 stick) dairy-free margarine
¼ cup silken tofu, blended until smooth
1 teaspoon vanilla
½ cup solid-pack pumpkin
2 cups old-fashioned oats
1 cup dried cranberries (optional)

1. Preheat oven to 350°F. Line cookie sheets with parchment paper. Sift flour, cinnamon, salt, nutmeg and baking soda into medium bowl.

2. Beat brown sugar and margarine in large bowl with electric mixer at medium speed about 5 minutes or until light and fluffy. Add tofu; beat until well blended. Beat in vanilla. Add pumpkin; beat at low speed until blended. Beat in flour mixture just until blended. Add oats; mix well. Stir in cranberries, if desired. Drop dough by rounded tablespoonfuls 2 inches apart onto prepared cookie sheets.

3. Bake 12 minutes or until golden brown. Cool on cookie sheets 1 minute; remove to wire racks to cool completely.

Makes about 2 dozen cookies

Whole Wheat Date Bars

4½ cups chopped dates
2½ cups water
2¾ cups whole wheat flour
2 cups old-fashioned oats
¼ cup all-purpose flour
¼ cup packed brown sugar
1½ teaspoons salt
½ teaspoon ground cinnamon
½ cup maple syrup
½ cup (1 stick) cold dairy-free margarine, cut into small pieces
1 cup vegetable shortening

1. Preheat oven to 400°F. Spray 13×9-inch baking pan with nonstick cooking spray.

2. Combine dates and water in large saucepan; cook and stir over medium heat 10 minutes or until thickened. Remove from heat.

3. Combine whole wheat flour, oats, all-purpose flour, brown sugar, salt and cinnamon in large bowl. Stir in maple syrup. Cut margarine into flour mixture with pastry blender or two knives until coarse crumbs form. Beat in shortening until dough holds together.

4. Place 5 cups dough in prepared pan; press firmly into bottom and partially up sides of pan to form crust. Pour date mixture evenly into crust. Crumble remaining dough over top.

5. Bake 25 minutes or until golden brown. Cool slightly in pan before cutting into bars.

Makes 2 dozen bars

Carrot Cake Cookies

1½ cups all-purpose flour
1 teaspoon ground cinnamon
½ teaspoon baking soda
½ teaspoon salt
¾ cup packed brown sugar
½ cup (1 stick) dairy-free margarine, softened
¼ cup canola oil
½ teaspoon vanilla
1 cup grated carrots (about 1 large)
½ cup chopped walnuts
½ cup raisins or chopped dried pineapple (optional)

1. Preheat oven to 350°F. Line cookie sheets with parchment paper. Combine flour, cinnamon, baking soda and salt in medium bowl.

2. Beat brown sugar and margarine in large bowl with electric mixer at medium speed about 3 minutes or until creamy. Add oil and vanilla; beat until well blended. Beat in flour mixture just until blended. Stir in carrots, walnuts and raisins, if desired. Drop dough by rounded tablespoonfuls 2 inches apart onto prepared cookie sheets.

3. Bake 12 to 14 minutes or until set and edges are lightly browned. Cool on cookie sheets 2 minutes; remove to wire racks to cool completely.

Makes about 2½ dozen cookies

Chocolate-Almond Crispy Treats

6 cups crisp brown rice cereal
1½ cups sliced almonds, toasted*
1 cup light corn syrup
⅓ cup almond butter
¼ cup packed brown sugar
3 tablespoons unsweetened cocoa powder
¼ teaspoon salt
1 cup semisweet chocolate chips

*To toast almonds, spread in single layer in heavy skillet. Cook over medium heat 1 to 2 minutes or until nuts are lightly browned, stirring frequently.

1. Line 13×9-inch baking pan with parchment paper; spray with nonstick cooking spray.

2. Combine rice cereal and almonds in large bowl.

3. Combine corn syrup, almond butter, brown sugar, cocoa and salt in large saucepan. Cook and stir over medium heat 5 minutes or until mixture is smooth and just begins to boil across surface.

4. Remove from heat; immediately stir cereal mixture into saucepan. Gently fold in chocolate chips. Press firmly into prepared pan. Let stand 1 hour or until set. Cut into bars.

Makes 2 dozen bars

Ginger Molasses Cookies

1 cup shortening
1 cup sugar
1 tablespoon baking soda
2 teaspoons ground ginger
2 teaspoons ground cinnamon
½ teaspoon salt
½ teaspoon ground nutmeg
½ teaspoon ground cloves
1 cup molasses
⅔ cup double-strength instant coffee*
Prepared egg replacer equal to 1 egg
4¾ cups all-purpose flour

To prepare double-strength coffee, follow instructions for instant coffee but use twice the recommended amount of instant coffee granules.

1. Preheat oven to 350°F. Line cookie sheets with parchment paper.

2. Beat shortening and sugar in large bowl with electric mixer at medium speed about 3 minutes or until creamy. Add baking soda, ginger, cinnamon, salt, nutmeg and cloves; beat until well blended. Add molasses, coffee and egg replacer, beating well after each addition. Gradually add flour, beating at low speed just until blended. Drop dough by tablespoonfuls 2 inches apart onto prepared cookie sheets.

3. Bake 12 to 15 minutes or until cookies are set but not browned. Cool on cookie sheets 1 minute; remove to wire racks to cool completely.

Makes about 4 dozen cookies

Peachy Oatmeal Bars

1½ cups all-purpose flour
1 cup old-fashioned oats
¾ cup (1½ sticks) dairy-free margarine, melted
½ cup sugar
1 teaspoon almond extract
½ teaspoon baking soda
¼ teaspoon salt
¾ cup peach preserves
⅓ cup flaked coconut

1. Preheat oven to 350°F. Spray 9-inch square baking pan with nonstick cooking spray.

2. Beat flour, oats, margarine, sugar, almond extract, baking soda and salt in large bowl with electric mixer at low speed 1 to 2 minutes or until crumbly. Reserve ¾ cup crumb mixture for topping; press remaining crumb mixture into bottom of prepared pan.

3. Spread peach preserves to within ½ inch of edges of pan; sprinkle with reserved crumb mixture and coconut.

4. Bake 22 to 27 minutes or until edges are lightly browned. Cool completely in pan on wire rack. Cut into bars.

Makes 16 bars

Maui Waui Cookies

> 2 cups all-purpose flour
> 1 cup quick oats
> ½ teaspoon baking powder
> ½ teaspoon salt
> ½ teaspoon ground cinnamon
> ¼ teaspoon baking soda
> 1 cup sugar
> 1 cup (2 sticks) dairy-free margarine, softened
>   Prepared egg replacer equal to 1 egg
> ¾ cup coarsely chopped salted macadamia nuts
> ½ cup flaked coconut
>   Pineapple Glaze (optional, recipe follows)

1. Preheat oven to 375°F. Line cookie sheets with parchment paper. Combine flour, oats, baking powder, salt, cinnamon and baking soda in small bowl.

2. Beat margarine and sugar in large bowl with electric mixer at medium-high speed about 3 minutes or until creamy. Beat in egg replacer. Beat in flour mixture at low speed, ½ cup at a time, until well blended. Stir in macadamia nuts and coconut. Drop dough by 2 tablespoonfuls about 2 inches apart onto prepared cookie sheets.

3. Bake 16 minutes or until cookies are set and edges are golden brown. Cool on cookie sheets 2 minutes; slide parchment paper with cookies onto wire racks to cool completely.

4. Prepare Pineapple Glaze, if desired; drizzle over cookies.

Makes about 3 dozen cookies

Pineapple Glaze: Place 1½ tablespoons melted dairy-free margarine in medium bowl. Stir in 1 cup powdered sugar until blended. Gradually add 4 to 6 teaspoons unsweetened pineapple juice until glaze reaches drizzling consistency.

Whole Wheat Brownies

½ cup whole wheat flour
½ teaspoon baking soda
¼ teaspoon salt
½ cup (1 stick) dairy-free margarine
1 cup packed brown sugar
½ cup unsweetened cocoa powder
½ cup silken tofu, stirred until smooth
½ cup semisweet chocolate chips
1 teaspoon vanilla

1. Preheat oven to 350°F. Spray 8-inch square baking pan with nonstick cooking spray. Combine flour, baking soda and salt in small bowl.

2. Melt margarine in large saucepan over low heat. Add brown sugar; cook and stir about 4 minutes or until sugar is completely dissolved and smooth. Remove pan from heat; sift in cocoa and stir until combined. Add flour mixture; stir until smooth. (Mixture will be thick.)

3. Beat in tofu until smooth. Stir in chocolate chips and vanilla. Pour batter into prepared pan.

4. Bake 25 minutes or until toothpick inserted into center comes out almost clean. Cool completely in pan on wire rack. Cut into squares or bars.

Makes 9 brownies

Crazy for Cake

Chocolate Fudge Mug Cake

3 tablespoons all-purpose flour
2 tablespoons granulated sugar
2 tablespoons packed brown sugar
2 tablespoons unsweetened cocoa powder
⅛ teaspoon baking powder
   Pinch salt
¼ cup vanilla soymilk
3 tablespoons dairy-free margarine, melted and cooled
¼ teaspoon vanilla
3 tablespoons semisweet chocolate chips
   Vanilla non-dairy frozen dessert (optional)

1. Combine flour, granulated sugar, brown sugar, cocoa, baking powder and salt in 12- to 16-ounce microwavable mug; mix well.

2. Combine soymilk, margarine and vanilla in small bowl; stir until blended (mixture will look curdled). Add to flour mixture; stir until well blended. Add chocolate chips; mix well.

3. Microwave on HIGH 1½ minutes. Let stand 3 to 4 minutes. Serve immediately. Top with frozen dessert, if desired.

Makes 1 to 2 servings

Peanut Butter Cupcakes

6 tablespoons water
2 tablespoons ground flaxseed
2 cups all-purpose flour
2 teaspoons baking powder
½ teaspoon baking soda
½ teaspoon salt
1 cup creamy peanut butter, divided
¼ cup (½ stick) dairy-free margarine, softened
1 cup packed brown sugar
1 cup vanilla soymilk
1½ cups mini semisweet chocolate chips, divided,
** plus additional for garnish**
Peanut Buttery Frosting (recipe follows)

1. Preheat oven to 350°F. Line 24 standard (2½-inch) muffin cups with paper baking cups.

2. Combine water and flaxseed in small saucepan; simmer over medium-low heat 5 minutes. Cool to room temperature.

3. Combine flour, baking powder, baking soda and salt in small bowl. Beat ½ cup peanut butter and margarine in large bowl with electric mixer at medium speed until blended. Add brown sugar; beat until well blended. Beat in flaxseed mixture. Add flour mixture alternately with soymilk; beat at low speed until well blended. Stir in 1 cup chocolate chips. Spoon batter evenly into prepared muffin cups.

4. Bake 15 minutes or until toothpick inserted into centers comes out clean. (Cover with foil if tops of cupcakes begin to brown too much.) Cool completely in pans on wire racks. Meanwhile, prepare frosting.

5. Pipe or spread frosting on cupcakes. Place remaining ½ cup peanut butter in small microwavable bowl; microwave on HIGH 15 seconds or until melted. Place remaining ½ cup chocolate chips in another microwavable bowl; microwave on HIGH 15 seconds or until melted. Drizzle peanut butter and chocolate over frosting. Garnish with additional chocolate chips.

Makes 24 cupcakes

Peanut Buttery Frosting: Beat ½ cup (1 stick) dairy-free margarine and ½ cup creamy peanut butter in medium bowl with electric mixer at medium speed until smooth. Gradually add 1½ cups sifted powdered sugar and 1 teaspoon vanilla until blended. Add 3 to 6 tablespoons vanilla soymilk, 1 tablespoon at a time, until smooth. Makes about 3 cups.

Easy Orange Cake

1½ cups all-purpose flour
1 cup sugar
Grated peel of 1 orange
1 teaspoon baking soda
¼ teaspoon salt
1 cup orange juice
5 tablespoons vegetable oil
Orange No-Butter Buttercream Frosting (recipe follows)
Candied orange peel (optional)

1. Preheat oven to 350°F. Spray 9-inch round cake pan with nonstick cooking spray.

2. Combine flour, sugar, orange peel, baking soda and salt in medium bowl. Combine orange juice and oil in small bowl or measuring cup. Add to flour mixture; stir until well blended. Spread batter in prepared pan.

3. Bake 30 minutes or until toothpick inserted into center comes out clean. Cool in pan on wire rack 5 minutes; remove to wire rack to cool completely. Meanwhile, prepare frosting.

4. Frost cake; garnish with orange peel.

Makes about 6 servings

Orange No-Butter Buttercream Frosting: Beat ½ cup (1 stick) dairy-free margarine in medium bowl with electric mixer at medium speed until light and fluffy. Beat in 2 tablespoons orange juice, 2 teaspoons grated orange peel and 1 teaspoon vanilla until blended. Gradually beat in 4 cups powdered sugar. Add 4 to 6 tablespoons soy creamer, 1 tablespoon at a time, until frosting is spreadable.

Banana Cupcakes

6 tablespoons water
2 tablespoons ground flaxseed
2 cups all-purpose flour
1½ cups granulated sugar
2 tablespoons packed brown sugar
2 teaspoons baking powder
½ teaspoon salt
½ teaspoon ground cinnamon
¼ teaspoon ground allspice
½ cup vegetable oil
½ cup vanilla soymilk
1 teaspoon vanilla
1 cup mashed bananas (about 2 medium)
1 container (16 ounces) dairy-free chocolate frosting
Chocolate sprinkles (optional)

1. Preheat oven to 350°F. Line 18 standard (2½-inch) muffin cups with paper baking cups.

2. Combine water and flaxseed in small saucepan; simmer over medium-low heat 5 minutes. Cool to room temperature.

3. Combine flour, granulated sugar, brown sugar, baking powder, salt, cinnamon and allspice in large bowl. Add oil, soymilk, vanilla and flaxseed mixture; beat with electric mixer at medium speed 2 minutes or until well blended. Beat in bananas until well blended. Spoon batter evenly into prepared muffin cups.

4. Bake 25 to 30 minutes or until toothpick inserted into centers comes out clean. Cool in pans on wire racks 10 minutes; remove to wire racks to cool completely.

5. Frost cupcakes; decorate with sprinkles, if desired.

Makes 18 cupcakes

Fudgy Chocolate Pudding Cake

  1 cup all-purpose flour
  1 cup granulated sugar, divided
  ½ cup unsweetened cocoa powder, divided
  2 teaspoons baking powder
  ¼ teaspoon salt
  ½ cup rice milk
  6 tablespoons dairy-free soy-free spread, melted
  1 teaspoon vanilla
  ⅔ cup packed dark brown sugar
  1¼ cups hot water
    Vanilla non-dairy frozen dessert (optional)

1. Preheat oven to 350°F. Spray 8-inch square baking pan with nonstick cooking spray.

2. Combine flour, ¾ cup granulated sugar, ¼ cup cocoa, baking powder and salt in medium bowl. Beat in rice milk, spread and vanilla until well blended. Pour batter into prepared pan.

3. Combine remaining ¼ cup granulated sugar, ¼ cup cocoa and brown sugar in small bowl; mix well. Sprinkle evenly over batter. Carefully pour hot water over batter. *Do not stir.*

4. Bake 25 to 35 minutes or until cake jiggles slightly when gently shaken. Let stand 15 minutes. Spoon into serving dishes; top with frozen dessert, if desired.

Makes 8 servings

Carrot Ginger Cupcakes

Cupcakes

9 tablespoons water

3 tablespoons ground flaxseed

3 cups all-purpose flour

⅓ cup coarsely chopped pecans, plus additional for garnish

2 teaspoons baking powder

1 teaspoon baking soda

1 teaspoon salt

½ teaspoon ground cinnamon

1½ cups granulated sugar

½ cup vegetable oil

½ cup (1 stick) dairy-free margarine, softened

1 tablespoon vanilla

1 pound carrots, shredded

Grated peel of 2 oranges

Juice of 1 orange

2 tablespoons grated fresh ginger

Frosting

½ cup (1 stick) dairy-free margarine

4½ cups powdered sugar

¼ cup orange juice

1 tablespoon grated fresh ginger

1 teaspoon vanilla

1. Preheat oven to 350°F. Line 24 standard (2½-inch) muffin cups with paper baking cups.

2. Combine water and flaxseed in small saucepan; simmer over medium-low heat 5 minutes. Cool to room temperature. Combine flour, ⅓ cup pecans, baking powder, baking soda, salt and cinnamon in medium bowl.

3. Beat granulated sugar, oil and ½ cup margarine in large bowl with electric mixer at medium speed until light and fluffy. Beat in flaxseed mixture and 1 tablespoon vanilla. Add carrots, orange peel, juice of one orange and 2 tablespoons ginger; mix well. Add flour mixture; mix just until combined. Spoon batter evenly into prepared muffin cups.

4. Bake 22 to 25 minutes or until toothpick inserted into centers comes out clean. Cool in pans on wire racks 10 minutes; remove to wire racks to cool completely.

5. For frosting, beat ½ cup margarine in large bowl with electric mixer at medium speed until creamy. Gradually add powdered sugar, beating well after each addition. Add ¼ cup orange juice, 1 tablespoon ginger and 1 teaspoon vanilla; beat at medium-high speed 1 minute or until well blended and fluffy.

6. Frost cupcakes; sprinkle with chopped pecans. Refrigerate until ready to serve.

Makes 24 cupcakes

Pear Spice Cake

> 4 cups chopped peeled pears
> 2 cups granulated sugar
> 1 cup chopped walnuts
> 6 tablespoons water
> 2 tablespoons ground flaxseed
> 3 cups all-purpose flour
> 2 teaspoons baking soda
> ¾ teaspoon ground cinnamon
> ½ teaspoon salt
> ¼ teaspoon ground nutmeg
> ⅛ teaspoon ground cloves
> 1 cup vegetable oil
> 1½ teaspoons vanilla
> Powdered sugar (optional)

1. Combine pears, granulated sugar and walnuts in medium bowl; mix lightly. Let stand 1 hour, stirring occasionally.

2. Preheat oven to 375°F. Grease and flour 12-cup (10-inch) bundt pan. Combine water and flaxseed in small saucepan; simmer over medium-low heat 5 minutes. Cool to room temperature.

3. Combine flour, baking soda, cinnamon, salt, nutmeg and cloves in medium bowl.

4. Beat flaxseed mixture, oil and vanilla in large bowl. Add flour mixture; mix well. Add pear mixture; mix well. Pour batter into prepared pan.

5. Bake 1 hour 10 minutes or until toothpick inserted near center comes out clean. Cool in pan on wire rack 20 minutes. Loosen edge of cake; invert onto rack to cool completely. Sprinkle with powdered sugar, if desired.

Makes 12 servings

Double Chocolate Cupcakes

1 cup all-purpose flour
½ cup unsweetened cocoa powder
1 teaspoon baking soda
½ teaspoon salt
1 cup soymilk
1½ teaspoons cider vinegar
¾ cup granulated sugar
⅓ cup vegetable oil
1 teaspoon vanilla
¼ cup semisweet chocolate chips
Powdered sugar

1. Preheat oven to 350°F. Line 10 standard (2¾-inch) muffin cups with paper baking cups or spray with nonstick cooking spray.

2. Sift flour, cocoa powder, baking soda and salt into small bowl. Combine soymilk and vinegar in large bowl; let stand 2 minutes.

3. Add sugar, oil and vanilla to soymilk mixture; whisk until foamy. Gradually add flour mixture, whisking until smooth. Stir in chocolate chips. Spoon batter evenly into prepared muffin cups.

4. Bake 15 to 18 minutes or until toothpick inserted into centers comes out clean. Cool in pans on wire racks 10 minutes; remove to wire racks to cool completely. Sprinkle with powdered sugar before serving.

Makes 10 cupcakes

Frosted Spiced Sweet Potato Cake

6 tablespoons water

2 tablespoons ground flaxseed

1½ cups all-purpose flour

1¼ cups granulated sugar

2 teaspoons baking powder

1 teaspoon ground cinnamon

½ teaspoon baking soda

½ teaspoon salt

¼ teaspoon ground allspice

1 can (29 ounces) sweet potatoes, drained and mashed

¾ cup canola oil

½ cup chopped walnuts, plus additional for garnish

½ cup raisins

Orange No-Butter Buttercream Frosting (page 234, optional)

1. Preheat oven to 325°F. Spray 13×9-inch baking pan with nonstick cooking spray. Combine water and flaxseed in small saucepan; simmer over medium-low heat 5 minutes. Cool to room temperature.

2. Combine flour, granulated sugar, baking powder, cinnamon, baking soda, salt and allspice in medium bowl. Beat mashed sweet potatoes, oil and flaxseed mixture in large bowl with electric mixer at low speed until blended. Add flour mixture; beat at medium speed 30 seconds or until well blended. Stir in ½ cup walnuts and raisins. Spread batter in prepared pan.

3. Bake 35 to 40 minutes or until toothpick inserted into center comes out clean. Cool completely in pan on wire rack.

4. Prepare frosting, if desired, omitting orange juice and orange peel. Spread frosting over cake; sprinkle with additional walnuts.

Makes 24 servings

Oat Apricot Snack Cake

1½ cups all-purpose flour
1 teaspoon baking soda
1 teaspoon ground cinnamon
½ teaspoon salt
1 container (6 ounces) plain soy yogurt
¾ cup packed brown sugar
½ cup granulated sugar
⅓ cup vegetable oil
¼ cup silken tofu, stirred until smooth
4 tablespoons orange juice, divided
2 teaspoons vanilla
2 cups old-fashioned oats
1 cup chopped dried apricots
1 cup powdered sugar

1. Preheat oven to 350°F. Spray 13×9-inch baking pan with nonstick cooking spray.

2. Combine flour, baking soda, cinnamon and salt in medium bowl. Whisk yogurt, brown sugar, granulated sugar, oil, tofu, 2 tablespoons orange juice and vanilla in large bowl. Add flour mixture; stir until blended. Stir in oats and apricots. Spread batter in prepared pan.

3. Bake 20 to 25 minutes or until toothpick inserted into center comes out clean. Cool completely in pan on wire rack.

4. Whisk powdered sugar and remaining 2 tablespoons orange juice in small bowl until smooth. Drizzle glaze over cake.

Makes 24 servings

Cool & Creamy

Avocado Lime Pops

1 avocado, peeled and pitted
1 cup sugar
1 cup dairy-free milk
   Juice and grated peel of 2 limes
¼ teaspoon vanilla
6 (5-ounce) plastic cups or paper cups or pop molds
6 pop sticks

1. Combine avocado, sugar, dairy-free milk, lime juice, lime peel and vanilla in blender or food processor; blend until smooth.

2. Pour mixture into cups. Cover top of each cup with small piece of foil. Freeze 1 hour.

3. Insert sticks through center of foil. Freeze 4 hours or until firm.

4. To serve, remove foil and gently twist frozen pops out of plastic cups or peel away paper cups.

Makes 6 pops

Intense Chocolate Ice Cream

2 cups plain rice milk, divided
¼ cup tapioca flour
¼ cup unsweetened cocoa powder
6 tablespoons sugar
¼ teaspoon salt
⅓ cup semisweet chocolate chips
½ teaspoon vanilla
  Fresh berries (optional)

1. Whisk ½ cup rice milk, tapioca flour and cocoa in medium saucepan until smooth. Add remaining 1½ cups rice milk; mix well. Stir in sugar and salt until blended. Cook over medium heat, stirring constantly, until mixture thickens to consistency of pudding. Remove from heat; stir in chocolate chips and vanilla until chocolate is melted and mixture is smooth.

2. Transfer to medium bowl; cover and refrigerate 2 hours or until cold.

3. Pour mixture into ice cream maker; process according to manufacturer's directions. Serve with berries, if desired.

Makes 4 servings

Green Tea Lychee Frappé

1 can (15 ounces) lychees in syrup,* undrained
2 cups water
2 slices peeled fresh ginger (2×¼ inches)
3 green tea bags
   Fresh orange slices and cherries (optional)

*Canned lychees are readily available in either the canned fruit or ethnic foods section of most large supermarkets.

1. Drain lychees, reserving syrup. Place lychees in single layer in medium resealable food storage bag; freeze 1 hour or until firm. Cover syrup and refrigerate.

2. Bring water and ginger to a boil in small saucepan over medium-high heat. Pour over tea bags in teapot or 2-cup heatproof measuring cup; steep 3 minutes. Discard ginger and tea bags. Cover tea and refrigerate until cool.

3. Combine frozen lychees, chilled green tea and ½ cup reserved syrup in blender or food processor; blend 20 seconds or until smooth.

4. Pour into two glasses. Garnish with orange slices and cherries. Serve immediately.

Makes 2 (10-ounce) servings

Note: Lychees are a subtropical fruit grown in China, Mexico and the United States. They are small oval fruit with rough, bright red hulls. Beneath the hull is milky white flesh surrounding a single seed. The flesh is sweet and juicy. Fresh lychees are available in Asian markets in the United States in early summer.

Bellini Pops

1 ripe peach, peeled and chopped (about 1 cup)
4 teaspoons sugar
1 tablespoon orange liqueur
1½ teaspoons fresh lemon juice
½ cup dry white wine
6 (2-ounce) paper or plastic cups
6 pop sticks

1. Place peach in blender or food processor; blend until smooth.

2. Combine peach, sugar, orange liqueur and lemon juice in small bowl. Stir in wine until well blended.

3. Pour mixture into cups. Cover top of each cup with small piece of foil. Freeze 2 hours.

4. Insert sticks through center of foil. Freeze 4 hours or until firm.

5. To serve, remove foil and gently twist frozen pops out of plastic cups or peel away paper cups. (Do not twist or pull sticks.)

Makes 6 pops

Coconut Milk Ice Cream ❯

2 cans (about 13 ounces each) unsweetened coconut milk
½ cup sugar
1 dairy-free candy bar, crushed into small pieces

1. Combine coconut milk and sugar in medium saucepan. Cook over medium-low heat, whisking constantly, until smooth and sugar is dissolved. Refrigerate until cold.

2. Pour mixture into ice cream maker; process according to manufacturer's directions, adding candy pieces during last 2 minutes. Transfer to freezer container; freeze until firm.

3. To serve, let ice cream soften at room temperature or microwave 20 to 30 seconds on HIGH.

Makes about 1 quart

Speedy Pineapple-Lime Sorbet

1 ripe pineapple, cut into cubes (about 4 cups)
⅓ cup frozen limeade concentrate
1 to 2 tablespoons fresh lime juice
1 teaspoon grated lime peel

1. Arrange pineapple in single layer on large baking sheet; freeze at least 1 hour or until very firm.*

2. Combine frozen pineapple, limeade concentrate, lime juice and lime peel in food processor or blender; process until smooth and fluffy. If mixture doesn't become smooth and fluffy, let stand 30 minutes to soften slightly; repeat processing. Serve immediately.

Pineapple can be frozen up to 1 month in resealable freezer food storage bags.

Makes 8 servings

Strawberry Lemonade Pops

**½ (12-ounce) can frozen lemonade concentrate,
  partly thawed**
1 cup ice
½ cup water
½ cup sliced strawberries
6 (3-ounce) paper or plastic cups or pop molds
6 pop sticks

1. Combine lemonade concentrate, ice, water and strawberries in blender or food processor; blend until smooth.

2. Pour mixture into cups. Cover top of each cup with small piece of foil. Freeze 1 hour.

3. Insert sticks through center of foil. Freeze 4 hours or until firm.

4. To serve, remove foil and peel away paper cups or gently twist frozen pops out of plastic cups.

Makes 6 pops

Strawberry Raspberry Lemonade Pops: Substitute raspberry lemonade concentrate for regular lemonade concentrate.

Cantaloupe Sorbet 〉

6 cups cubed fresh cantaloupe
⅓ cup light corn syrup
3 tablespoons lime juice

1. Place cantaloupe in food processor; process until smooth. Add corn syrup and lime juice; process until well blended. Transfer to medium bowl; refrigerate until cold.

2. Pour mixture into ice cream maker; process according to manufacturer's directions.

Makes 4 cups (8 servings)

Dairy-Free Pudding Ice Cream

1 package (8-serving size) instant pudding and
**   pie filling mix***
3 cups dairy-free milk
**   Optional additions: nuts, chocolate chips or**
**   crushed candies**

*Choose any dairy-free flavor, but check ingredient lists. Not all are dairy-free.

1. Whisk pudding mix and dairy-free milk in large bowl until smooth. Immediately transfer to ice cream maker; process according to manufacturers directions.

2. Serve immediately or transfer to freezer container. If frozen solid, let ice cream stand at room temperature to soften before serving.

Makes about 6 servings

Orange Granita

6 small Valencia or blood oranges
¼ cup sugar
¼ cup water
⅛ teaspoon ground cinnamon

1. Cut oranges in half; squeeze juice into medium bowl and reserve empty shells. Strain juice to remove seeds, if necessary.

2. Combine sugar and water in small microwavable bowl; microwave on HIGH 30 seconds to 1 minute or until sugar is dissolved. Stir sugar mixture and cinnamon into orange juice.

3. Pour juice mixture into shallow 9-inch baking pan. Cover and place on flat surface in freezer. After 1 to 2 hours when ice crystals form at edges, stir with fork. Stir two or three more times at 20- to 30-minute intervals until granita has texture of icy snow.

4. Serve granita in orange shells.

Makes 6 servings

Variations: Add a small amount of orange liqueur to the orange juice mixture before freezing. Garnish with dairy-free whipped topping and a candied orange slice.

Tropic Pops

2 bananas, cut into chunks
1½ cups unsweetened coconut milk
1½ cups pineapple juice
2 tablespoons sugar
½ teaspoon vanilla
⅛ teaspoon ground nutmeg
¼ cup flaked coconut
8 (5-ounce) plastic or paper cups or pop molds
8 pop sticks

1. Combine bananas, coconut milk, pineapple juice, sugar, vanilla and nutmeg in blender or food processor; blend until smooth. Stir in coconut.

2. Pour mixture into cups. Cover top of each cup with small piece of foil. Freeze 2 hours.

3. Insert sticks through center of foil. Freeze 6 hours or until firm.

4. To serve, remove foil and gently twist pops out of plastic cups or peel away paper cups.

Makes 8 pops

Fruit Finales

Mixed Berry Crisp

6 cups mixed berries, thawed if frozen
¾ cup packed brown sugar, divided
¼ cup quick-cooking tapioca
Juice of ½ lemon
1 teaspoon ground cinnamon
½ cup all-purpose flour
6 tablespoons cold dairy-free margarine, cut into small pieces
½ cup sliced almonds

1. Preheat oven to 375°F. Spray 8- or 9-inch square baking pan with nonstick cooking spray.

2. Combine berries, ¼ cup brown sugar, tapioca, lemon juice and cinnamon in large bowl; mix well. Pour into prepared pan.

3. For topping, combine flour, remaining ½ cup brown sugar and butter in food processor; pulse until mixture resembles coarse crumbs. Add almonds; pulse until combined. (Leave some large pieces of almonds.) Sprinkle over berry mixture.

4. Bake 20 to 30 minutes or until golden brown.

Makes about 9 servings

Peaches and Cinnamon Rice Pudding

1 cup water
⅓ cup uncooked rice (not converted)
1 tablespoon dairy-free margarine
⅛ teaspoon salt
1 can (16 ounces) sliced peaches in unsweetened
    juice, undrained
½ cup dairy-free milk, divided
2 teaspoons cornstarch
½ teaspoon ground cinnamon
¼ cup peach fruit spread, plus additional for topping
    Dairy-free whipped topping (optional)

1. Combine water, rice, margarine and salt in medium saucepan; bring to a boil over high heat. Reduce heat to low; cover and simmer 25 minutes or until rice is tender. Remove from heat.

2. Drain canned peaches, reserving ½ cup juice. Set peaches aside. Stir reserved juice and ¼ cup dairy-free milk into cooked rice.

3. Combine cornstarch and cinnamon in medium bowl; mix well. Gradually add remaining ¼ cup dairy-free milk, stirring until smooth. Add to rice mixture; bring to a boil over medium-high heat, stirring constantly. Reduce heat to low; simmer 2 minutes or until thickened, stirring frequently. Remove from heat; stir in ¼ cup peach spread. Cool to room temperature, stirring occasionally.

4. Chop drained peaches; stir into pudding. Spoon pudding into four dessert dishes. Serve at room temperature or chilled. Garnish with whipped topping and additional peach spread, if desired.

Makes 4 servings

Almond-Pear Strudel

¾ cup slivered almonds
5 to 6 cups thinly sliced crisp pears (4 to 5 medium)
1 tablespoon grated lemon peel
1 tablespoon lemon juice
⅓ cup plus 1 teaspoon sugar, divided
2 teaspoons ground cinnamon
1 teaspoon ground nutmeg
6 sheets (¼ pound) phyllo dough
¼ cup (½ stick) dairy-free margarine, melted
½ teaspoon almond extract
   Powdered sugar

1. Preheat oven to 300°F. Spread almonds in shallow baking pan. Bake 6 to 8 minutes or until lightly browned, stirring frequently.

2. Combine pears, lemon peel and lemon juice in large microwavable bowl; microwave on HIGH 6 minutes or until tender; set aside to cool. Combine ⅓ cup sugar, cinnamon and nutmeg in small bowl.

3. Cover work surface with plastic wrap. Place one phyllo sheet in center of plastic wrap. (Cover remaining phyllo dough with damp kitchen towel to prevent dough from drying out.) Brush phyllo with 1 teaspoon margarine. Top with second sheet of phyllo; brush with 1 teaspoon margarine. Repeat layers with remaining phyllo dough.

4. *Increase oven temperature to 400°F.* Spray baking sheet with nonstick cooking spray. Drain pears; toss with sugar mixture and almond extract.

5. Spread pear mixture evenly over phyllo, leaving 3-inch strip on far long side. Sprinkle pears with ½ cup almonds. Brush strip with 2 teaspoons butter. Beginning with long side of phyllo closest to you, carefully roll up jelly-roll style, using plastic wrap to gently lift dough. Place strudel, seam side down, on prepared baking sheet. Brush with 1 teaspoon margarine.

6. Bake 20 minutes or until golden brown. Brush with remaining margarine; sprinkle with remaining ¼ cup almonds and 1 teaspoon sugar. Bake 5 minutes. Cool 10 minutes before serving.

Makes 8 servings

Lemon-Ginger Apple Crisp

6 cups peeled apple slices

¼ cup plus 2 tablespoons packed brown sugar, divided

3 tablespoons all-purpose flour, divided

2 tablespoons lemon juice

1 teaspoon grated lemon peel

½ teaspoon ground ginger

¼ cup quick oats

1 tablespoon dairy-free margarine, melted

1. Preheat oven to 350°F. Combine apples, ¼ cup brown sugar, 1 tablespoon flour, lemon juice, lemon peel and ginger in 2-quart ovenproof microwavable baking dish; toss to coat.

2. Combine remaining 2 tablespoons brown sugar, 2 tablespoons flour, oats and margarine in small bowl; mix well. Sprinkle evenly over apple mixture.

3. Microwave on HIGH 12 to 15 minutes or until mixture begins to bubble.

4. Bake 15 to 20 minutes or until apples are tender and topping is golden brown.

Makes 6 servings

Peachy Keen Dessert Treat ❯

1⅓ cups old-fashioned oats
1 cup *each* granulated sugar and packed brown sugar
⅔ cup buttermilk baking mix
2 teaspoons ground cinnamon
½ teaspoon ground nutmeg
2 pounds fresh peaches (about 8 medium), sliced

Slow Cooker Directions

Combine oats, granulated sugar, brown sugar, baking mix, cinnamon and nutmeg in large bowl. Stir in peaches until blended. Pour mixture into slow cooker. Cover; cook on LOW 4 to 6 hours.

Makes 8 to 12 servings

Cabernet Pears

4 Bosc pears, peeled and cored, stems attached
1 bottle (750 mL) Carbernet Sauvignon
Water
⅓ cup plus ¼ cup sugar, divided
1 stick cinnamon
7 peppercorns
1 bay leaf
2 whole cloves
3 sprigs fresh thyme

1. Place pears in large saucepan. Pour in wine; add water as needed to cover pears. Add ⅓ cup sugar, cinnamon, peppercorns, bay leaf, cloves and thyme; bring to a boil. Reduce heat to low; simmer, uncovered, 35 minutes or until pears are fork-tender.

2. Remove pears to serving dish. Strain 2 cups liquid into medium saucepan and add remaining ¼ cup sugar. Bring to a boil; cook 15 to 30 minutes or until reduced to a sauce. Serve over pears.

Makes 4 servings

Strawberry Rhubarb Crumble

4 cups sliced rhubarb (1-inch pieces)
3 cups sliced strawberries (about 1 pint)
¾ cup granulated sugar
⅓ cup plus ¼ cup all-purpose flour, divided
1 tablespoon grated lemon peel
1 cup quick oats
½ cup packed brown sugar
½ teaspoon ground cinnamon
½ teaspoon salt
⅓ cup dairy-free margarine, melted

1. Preheat oven to 375°F. Combine rhubarb and strawberries in large bowl.

2. Combine granulated sugar, ¼ cup flour and lemon peel in small bowl. Sprinkle over fruit; toss to coat. Transfer to 9-inch square baking pan.

3. Combine oats, brown sugar, remaining ⅓ cup flour, cinnamon and salt in medium bowl. Stir in margarine until mixture is crumbly. Sprinkle over rhubarb mixture.

4. Bake 45 to 50 minutes or until filling is bubbly and topping is lightly browned. Serve warm or at room temperature.

Makes 8 servings

Metric Conversion Chart

VOLUME MEASUREMENTS (dry)

$1/8$ teaspoon = 0.5 mL
$1/4$ teaspoon = 1 mL
$1/2$ teaspoon = 2 mL
$3/4$ teaspoon = 4 mL
1 teaspoon = 5 mL
1 tablespoon = 15 mL
2 tablespoons = 30 mL
$1/4$ cup = 60 mL
$1/3$ cup = 75 mL
$1/2$ cup = 125 mL
$2/3$ cup = 150 mL
$3/4$ cup = 175 mL
1 cup = 250 mL
2 cups = 1 pint = 500 mL
3 cups = 750 mL
4 cups = 1 quart = 1 L

VOLUME MEASUREMENTS (fluid)

1 fluid ounce (2 tablespoons) = 30 mL
4 fluid ounces ($1/2$ cup) = 125 mL
8 fluid ounces (1 cup) = 250 mL
12 fluid ounces ($1 1/2$ cups) = 375 mL
16 fluid ounces (2 cups) = 500 mL

WEIGHTS (mass)

$1/2$ ounce = 15 g
1 ounce = 30 g
3 ounces = 90 g
4 ounces = 120 g
8 ounces = 225 g
10 ounces = 285 g
12 ounces = 360 g
16 ounces = 1 pound = 450 g

DIMENSIONS

$1/16$ inch = 2 mm
$1/8$ inch = 3 mm
$1/4$ inch = 6 mm
$1/2$ inch = 1.5 cm
$3/4$ inch = 2 cm
1 inch = 2.5 cm

OVEN TEMPERATURES

250°F = 120°C
275°F = 140°C
300°F = 150°C
325°F = 160°C
350°F = 180°C
375°F = 190°C
400°F = 200°C
425°F = 220°C
450°F = 230°C

BAKING PAN SIZES

Utensil	Size in Inches/Quarts	Metric Volume	Size in Centimeters
Baking or Cake Pan (square or rectangular)	8×8×2	2 L	20×20×5
	9×9×2	2.5 L	23×23×5
	12×8×2	3 L	30×20×5
	13×9×2	3.5 L	33×23×5
Loaf Pan	8×4×3	1.5 L	20×10×7
	9×5×3	2 L	23×13×7
Round Layer Cake Pan	8×1½	1.2 L	20×4
	9×1½	1.5 L	23×4
Pie Plate	8×1¼	750 mL	20×3
	9×1¼	1 L	23×3
Baking Dish or Casserole	1 quart	1 L	—
	1½ quarts	1.5 L	—
	2 quarts	2 L	—